THE QUICK & EASY MICROWAVE OVEN COOKBOOK

THE QUICK & EASY MICROWAVE OVEN COOKBOOK

BY GINGER SCRIBNER

BROOKE HOUSE • LOS ANGELES, CALIFORNIA

Manufactured in the United States of America

Library of Congress Cataloging in Publication Data

Scribner, Ginger.
The quick and easy microwave oven cookbook.

Includes index.
1. Microwave cookery. I. Title.
TX832.S4 641.5'88 75-34549
ISBN 0-912588-19-5

CONTENTS

ACKNOWLEDGMENTS

I wrote this book with the encouragement and help of many people. I would like to acknowledge and thank the following for their assistance.

Jess Bateman read the technical parts. He has worked with microwave for the last four years of his 28-year electrical career; his electrical inventions include the microlite (page 6).

Judy Davis racked her brain with me over certain aspects of the recipes. She has a Bachelor of Arts in Home Economics from California State University at Fresno, California, and has worked five years as a home economist and two years as a consumer services consultant.

Karen Sweeney, free-lance writer and good friend, read my first draft.

Melvin Hull, my step-father, shared his recipe collection with me—special thanks to him. He has served 15 years on the board of the Southern California Restaurant Association.

Vivian Hull, my mother, and Myrtle Webster, my mother-in-law, shared their family recipes.

Marlene Scherzberg went through her personal recipe files and loaded me down with good ideas.

Dennis Duskin and Shawn Scribner, both fifteen, helped test the recipes and washed hundreds of dirty dishes—a big thank you to them.

Lastly, Neal, my husband, and Kent, Shawn, Blake, and Todd, my sons, endured eating many of my recipes. Shawn deserves special notice as he ate 12 pies in one week and asked for more!

THE QUICK & EASY MICROWAVE OVEN COOKBOOK

INTRODUCTION

If Adam and Eve sold themselves for an apple, what would they have done for a microwave oven? To me, quick cooking is necessary to a fun-loving, casual life-style. The working husband or wife can enjoy new freedom through the incredible cooking speed of microwaves. Singles can eat family-style meals without fuss and fanfare.

Do you want to impress someone special? Cook lobster tail in two and one-half to three minutes; bake potatoes in eight minutes. Let your friend toss a salad. Suddenly you'll have lots of time to get acquainted.

There are times when microwave cooking resembles a gift from the Fairy Godmother. One morning I was awakened at 6:30 as cars descended on our circular driveway like picnic ants marching to honey. I poked my husband and exclaimed, "We're being invaded!" "Oh," he mumbled, "I forgot to tell you. I invited everyone in the golf tournament to drop by for breakfast." "Breakfast!" I screamed. After jumping out of bed, I flew into the kitchen, opened the freezer, grabbed an armful of rolls and breads, and—you guessed it—threw them into my microwave oven. In fifteen minutes, the new Cinderella served warm rolls, hot coffee, and scrambled eggs on paper plates to all the golfers.

When microwave ovens came on the market in force in the mid-1960s, I knew they were for me. The first patent, titled "Treating Foodstuffs," was filed in 1945; it was a spinoff from radar development. Of course microwave ovens have come a long way since then. The term "oven" is actually a misnomer because this cooking accessory performs many typical surface-unit jobs as well as oven cookery.

Microwave cooking usually cuts cooking time in half. "Standing time" for the food is an important difference. This is usually necessary because the temperature of the food rises after it leaves the oven—the food continues to cook. The "standing time" varies depending on the density and volume of the food.

You may find that combining the range top or conventional oven methods with microwave methods is a convenient way to treat certain recipes. Using this process, you may not always cook in half the time, but you will certainly speed things up.

There are times when there is little advantage in using the microwave oven. For foods that need to rehydrate, you have to allow for the same amount of time in the microwave oven as you do when cooking conventionally. Two examples are pastas and rice.

The microwave cooking method does three things: *cooks, defrosts,* and *reheats.* Cooking, of course, is what this book is all about. Whether you cook for a couple or a crowd, you'll save time using microwave cooking.

The recipes and instructions in this book will help you prepare foods that look and taste like gourmet cooking; however, only you'll know they are made from delicious convenience foods. These pre-prepared items are used to achieve the flavor formerly attained only by long hours in the kitchen. Let other people sift, measure, stir, and simmer for you. Be inventive with the flavors of pre-prepared items and alter them to suit your own personality and taste.

Be sure your family or guests are ready to eat when you set the dial because instant foods and microwave ovens have made it possible to spend less time preparing dinner than getting the diners to the table.

Because consumer microwave units are relatively new on the market, prospective buyers, and even veteran owners, have many questions. Here I will answer the most common ones.

How Does the Oven Work?

Microwave cooking is completely unlike other methods. All you need to do is set the timer and let the microwaves cook for you. The following explains simply how the miracle microwave oven works.

Because microwave ovens use airwaves, the United States Communications Commission controls the frequency; the commission assigned 915, 2450, 15,800, and 22,125 Megahertz to microwave ovens. Microwaves within these wavelength bands have two features important to food cooking. If a lower frequency were used, the heating rate would be slower; a higher frequency would concentrate heat on the surface only. Also, the dimensions needed for the ovens are of a practical size for the wavebands (12-1/2 inches for 915 MHz and 5 inches for 2450 MHz). The waves are transmitted through space and through a wave guide with great accuracy.

Microwave ovens have a magnetron tube (similar to a vacuum tube) that generates electromagnetic waves—a high energy frequency. The waves are either *reflected, transmitted,* or *absorbed.* Foods absorb; papers, glass, and many plastics transmit; and metals reflect. A mode stirrer distributes the wave pattern as it feeds into the oven so that foods cook evenly.

How Does the Food Cook?

The food does not cook in the conventional "heating-the-air" process; it cooks itself. Microwaves are transmitted from the magnetron in the top of the oven and bounce off the metal walls in an even pattern to cook the food uniformly. They travel through the food container to the food, where they cause the liquid food molecules to vibrate against each other. This friction creates heat to cook the food.

There is a depth-of-penetration effect as energy is absorbed by the food. The intensity of the fields diminishes from surface to interior; a significant difference can be found between the outside surface and the center. This action is negligible for thin food items.

Is It Safe?

Yes. Microwaves are classified as non-ionizing; they are a low level form of radiant energy similar to light, radio waves, and infrared heat. Also, the United States Department of Health, Education, and Welfare established stringent safety standards in 1971 and 1974. Look for the HEW seal on the oven. Safety features are interlocks on the doors to turn the oven off when the door is open, special door construction, and door seals to prevent most leakage. A small appliance called microlite tests leakage; you can purchase a microlite at hardware and appliance stores.

How Nutritious Is It?

Microwave cooking is the best way to save the nutritional content of food. Lower surface temperature and shorter cooking time minimize the breakdown of food nutrients and their subsequent evaporation. Since you cook vegetables and fruits dry, they retain their vitamins instead of leaving them in cooking water. The delicate color and flavors of many foods, such as casseroles, poultry, and fish, are similarly enhanced by microwave cooking.

What Is the Operating Cost?

Running a microwave oven costs less than running a conventional one. A microwave oven uses about half the power, and the shorter cooking time makes it less expensive to use than your regular oven.

How to Use Convenience Foods

Remove foil lids. Use only foil containers about 3/4 inch in depth. NEVER SET A FOIL CONTAINER DIRECTLY ON THE MICROWAVE OVEN CAVITY BASE OR LET IT TOUCH THE CAVITY SIDES. Instead, set a foil container on a paper towel. FOLLOW YOUR MANUFACTURER'S INSTRUCTIONS FOR THE USE OF METAL.

Loosen a frozen meat or vegetable pie and place it in a bowl approximately the size of the pie. If you are really in a hurry and can't use any metal, put all the ingredients on a paper plate or a divided plastic picnic plate.

You can use paper towels, napkins, wax paper, or paper plates interchangeably for all items that cook on paper goods.

A convenience foods guide accompanies each food section in this book.

Pantry and Freezer Supplies

A whole world of convenience foods and flavors, covered and encased in bottles, boxes, and other containers, are just waiting to be unveiled in your kitchen. The philosophy of this book is that these convenience foods should be used often with vim, vigor, and creative genius. Most of the pantry and freezer supplies are listed in the convenience food guides accompanying each food section. Make sure you have a good supply of the listed items on hand for quick and easy cooking.

Artichoke Hearts, marinated and plain, canned or frozen
Barbecue Sauce
Boxed Mixes (all kinds)
Bread Crumbs
Catsup
Chili
Chili Sauce
Chives, frozen
Chutney
Croutons
Dehydrated Salad Mixes
Dehydrated Seasoning Mixes
Dried Fruits
Garlic Spread
Grated Parmesan and Romano Cheese, canned
Herbs and Spices
Horseradish
Hot Dog Sauce
Instant Coffee, Sanka, and Tea
Juices, canned and frozen
Kitchen Bouquet (bottled browning sauce)
Liquid Smoke
Liquor
Marshmallows
Mayonnaise
Nuts and Seeds
Oil, olive and vegetable
Olives, brown and green, chopped and whole
Onions, instant minced
Pepper Flakes, sweet
Peppercorns
Pickles
Prepared Mustard
Relishes
Salad Dressings
Soft Drinks
Soy Sauce
Sweet-and-Sour Sauce
Tabasco Sauce
Teriyaki Sauce
Tomato Paste, Puree, and Sauce
Vinegar, white and wine
Worcestershire Sauce

How to Use the Recipes

These recipes are for quick and easy cooking; therefore, feel free to substitute any dried, dehydrated, frozen, and canned products for the real thing. Part or all of the ingredients can be substituted in any recipe. You will have to adjust your oven cooking time, normally by two or three minutes only.

Canned Foods: Remember these are already cooked; they need only to be heated.

Dehydrated Products: Instant minced onion and sweet pepper flakes are used for convenience and speed in preparing the recipes. Freshly cut chopped or minced onion and green pepper are always better. Grated lemon and orange peel are far superior to dried ones.

Herbs: Again, for convenience and practicality, commercial dried herbs are used. If you use fresh ones, double the amount or to taste.

Weight: Different food product brands may have various weights for the same size container. Use the weight nearest to that given in the recipe. A difference of one or two ounces will not change the taste.

Cooking Time

Conventional methods don't apply! The amount of time needed to cook your food is directly related to the size, amount, starting temperature, and density of the food. One small potato takes slightly less time to cook than one large potato. As you place more items in the oven, you need to adjust the cooking time; more items need more time. One medium potato needs 3 minutes 30 seconds, but six medium potatoes need 15-16 minutes. Frozen items such as a ten-ounce box of vegetables take about two to three minutes more cooking time than the same items defrosted. High density food items need more cooking time. A one-pound roast needs to cook longer than a one-pound squash.

All microwave ovens are not alike. Some have more cooking power (watts) than others; the cavity size varies with each manufacturer; and they are put together with varying degrees of technical skill. Therefore, the cooking times listed in this book are close approximations. My oven is approximately 16 x 15 x 9 inches; the wattage is 600. You must experiment with your own oven and adjust the recipes accordingly.

After being removed from the microwave oven, food cooks by thermal heat if kept covered. Once, when I cooked brownies for some guests, we sampled them right away. They were warm, moist, and delicious. Later, when we wanted a second helping, they were hard as rocks. Because someone had covered the container with a plate, the brownies had continued to cook.

To keep a food item such as a vegetable or meat warm, always cover it when you remove it from your oven. It will continue to cook a little, so adjust your cooking time to allow for this slight difference.

Don't stack food containers because the food won't cook evenly. Some containers need to be rotated about three or four times during the cooking process for best results.

Foods cooked by microwaves are tested for doneness in the same way you test conventionally cooked food. Pinch vegetables and fruit, or stick a fork into them. Use a toothpick to test batter-based recipes and custards. Stick a knife into meats, poultry, and fish. You can use a meat thermometer ONLY WHEN THE MEAT IS OUT OF THE MICROWAVE OVEN. The meat temperature rises after about five minutes standing time. Taste test is always a good method, but be sure the food has first cooled sufficiently.

Utensils

RETHINK IS THE MOTTO.

The most unusual food containers are used in the microwave oven. Common metal pots and pans cannot be used because the electromagnetic wave pattern is disturbed by metal. Even very small amounts of metal can cause "arcing" which pits the oven cavity. Early models may not allow any metal. Because metal reflects, microwaves might return through the wave guide to the megatron tube and ruin it. See metal exceptions (page 11).

Watch for utensils designed especially for microwave oven use. Microwave browning platters or skillets, bundt pans, round molds, and special thermometers are just a few of the new products you can purchase.

Plastic

Use plastic utensils to heat food, not to cook it.

1. Hard plastic bowls and trays
2. Styrofoam plastic plates and cups, with or without lids
3. Most plastic bowls that contain refrigerated, prepared products
4. Dishwasher proof products
5. Melamine ware (Test it first.)
6. Thermoses
7. Plastic wraps and bags

Cooking Pouch Bags

1. Frozen food plastic pouch bags (Cut a slit in the bag to allow steam to escape.)
2. Oven cooking bags (Follow manufacturer's directions.)

Paper Goods

1. Napkins
2. Towels
3. Cups
4. Plates
5. Cartons
6. Cardboards
7. Freezer Wraps
8. Bags

Glass, China, and Ceramic

1. Any container without metallic paint, designs, or attachments on them
2. Corning products are suitable except for Livingware, closed-handle cups, cook-n-serve covers, and Centura dinnerware.

Straw Baskets

1. Baskets to warm rolls

Wood

1. Small wooden utensils, such as spoons, for stirring
2. Don't use large wooden bowls or planks because the molecules in them will cook.

Metal Exceptions

Do not have metal in direct contact with the oven cavity. FOLLOW YOUR MANUFACTURER'S DIRECTIONS FOR THE USE OF ANY METAL. Many microwave ovens allow the following:

1. TV dinner trays if less than 3/4 inch deep
2. Metal skewers if completely covered by meats and/or vegetables
3. Jar lids, as for canning
4. Metal clamps
5. Aluminum foil in very small amounts as called for in recipes

Utensil Lids

1. Casserole lids
2. Paper towel, plastic wrap, and wax paper coverings (Make a small steam hole.)
3. Freezer wrap for a loose cover

Test

If you are not sure you should use the container you have chosen, test it.

1. Put the utensil in the microwave oven.
2. Set the time for 20 seconds.
3. If the container becomes hot, don't use it!
4. In case the container heats up, USE HOT PADS TO REMOVE IT FROM THE OVEN.

Cleaning the Oven

After each use, wipe up spills and splatters with water or a mild detergent; don't let food spillage build up. NEVER LET FOOD SPILLAGE BUILD UP AROUND THE MICROWAVE OVEN DOOR. Such excess crust could displace the tight door seal and allow microwaves to escape. Foods never get baked on as in a conventional oven, so cleaning the oven is easy. To get rid of odors, boil a cup of water and one tablespoon lemon juice or baking soda for three minutes in the oven.

DRINKS

"Chocolate is one of the most effective restoratives," said Brillat-Savarin. "All those who have to work when they might be sleeping, men of wit who feel temporarily deprived of their intellectual powers, those who find the weather oppressive, time dragging, the atmosphere depressing; those who are tormented by some preoccupation which deprives them of the liberty of thought; let all such men imbibe a half-litre of chocolate-umbre. . . ." If chocolate actually does all those marvelous things, no wonder there are so many chocolaholics! It is true that often nothing can beat a good cup of hot chocolate. The mix recipe on page 15 allows you to make the mix and then let everyone cook his own cup of chocolate in the microwave oven whenever he feels like it.

If you have a defrost or simmer dial, use it for all hot drinks once they have reached the boiling point; otherwise, you have to turn your oven on and off about every four to five minutes. Fill drink containers two-thirds full; this assures there is no hot liquid overflow.

I can't promise that all the drinks will suddenly make your intelligence quotient rise or turn you into a happy Pollyanna, but they all are delicious and fast to prepare. The Mexican Rompope on page 17 is especially good. This drink can't be sold in the United States, which, for me, is truly unfortunate because it is my favorite beverage. Since I didn't want to unlawfully cart Rompope over the border, I started a recipe search. Finally, in a Mexico City small bookstall situated in a cave-like room beneath a building, I found the recipe. As you will see, it is simplicity itself.

Drink Convenience Foods Guide

NAME	AMOUNT	DIRECTIONS	TIME
Cocoa Mix	1 cup	Heat milk. Put in chocolate and stir.	1 min. 15 sec., uncovered.
Coffee or Tea, Instant	1 cup	Heat water. Put in coffee or tea and stir.	1 min. 15 sec. to 2 min. 30 sec., uncovered.
Juices, Frozen	6 oz. can	Remove top. Heat to loosen.	15 sec., uncovered.
		Place in container. Heat to melt.	15 sec., uncovered.

CUPS	COOKING TIME
2	3 min. to 3 min. 30 sec.
3	4 min. to 4 min. 30 sec.
4	5 min. to 5 min. 30 sec.
5	6 min. 30 sec. to 7 min.
6	7 min. 30 sec. to 8 min. 30 sec.
7	9 min. to 9 min. 30 sec.
8	10 min. to 11 min.
9	12 min. to 13 min.
10	13 min. to 14 min.

Hot Bloody Mary

1 (46-ounce) can **tomato juice**
1 **cinnamon stick**
1/2 teaspoon **allspice**
1/4 teaspoon **cloves**
2 tablespoons **Worcestershire sauce**
3-10 drops **Tabasco sauce**
1 **beef bouillon cube**
4 cups **vodka**

1. In a tall, 3-quart container, combine all ingredients except vodka.

2. Cook 3 minutes, uncovered; stand 2 minutes. Repeat until juice has cooked 30 minutes.

3. Add vodka just before serving.

Makes about 10-11 cups.

Hot Brandied Pineapple-Apple Juice

1 (46-ounce) can **pineapple juice**
2 (46-ounce) cans **apple juice**
1/2 cup **red hots candies**
2 sticks **cinnamon**
1 cup **apple brandy** or to taste

1. In a 4-quart container, combine all ingredients except brandy.

2. Cook 5 minutes, uncovered; rest 5 minutes. Repeat until drink has cooked 30 minutes.

3. Add brandy just before serving.

Makes 20-22 cups.

Cappuccino

3 cups **milk**
6 tablespoons **instant coffee**
6 teaspoons **sugar**
3/4 cup **Galliano liqueur**
3 cups **water**

1. In a 1-quart container, cook milk 5 minutes.

2. Place 1 tablespoon instant coffee in each cup. Add the sugar and liqueur.

3. Add 1/2 cup milk to each cup. Stir. Add water to make a cup of liquid.

4. Place the 6 cups in a circular pattern; cook 5-6 minutes, uncovered.

Makes 6 cups.

Chocolate Pot of Cream

6 egg **yolks**
1/2 cup **sugar**
2 cups **cream,** heated
2 (6-ounce) packages **semisweet chocolate pieces**
1/2 cup **creme de menthe**
1 (7-ounce) can **pressurized whipped cream or 2 cups sweetened whipped cream**

1. In a bowl, beat egg yolks. For best results, use electric mixer.
2. Add sugar and beat until slightly thick.
3. Add cream; beat until smooth.
4. Pour mixture into a 1 1/2-quart container. Cook 4-5 minutes, uncovered. Stir every 15 seconds.
5. Mix in chocolate pieces. Stir until melted.
6. Add creme de menthe.
7. Pour mixture into 6 mugs or 12 demitasse cups. Refrigerate until cold.
8. When ready to serve, top with whipped cream.

Makes 6-12 cups.

Hot Chocolate Mix

2 pounds **instant chocolate mix**
1 (6-ounce) jar of **powdered cream**
1 cup **powdered sugar**
1 (8-quart) package **instant dry milk**

In a bowl, combine all ingredients and store in an airtight, 5-quart container.

Makes 213 servings.

One Cup

3 tablespoons **mix or to taste**
1 cup **water**

In a cup, add water to mix. Cook 2 minutes, uncovered.

South American Fruit Atoles

2 cups **water**
1-1/2 teaspoons **cornstarch**
4 cups **milk**
1-1/4 cups **sugar**
4 cups soft **fruit**, such as
  strawberries, bananas, peaches, apricots
1 cup **cream**
Fruit or **mint garnish**

1. In a 3-quart container, combine water and cornstarch. Stir to dissolve cornstarch. Cook 4 minutes, uncovered. Stir every 30 seconds.

2. Add milk and sugar. Cook 6 minutes, uncovered. Stir once.

3. Puree fruit and cream in a blender until smooth, or cut fruit in small pieces and push through a sieve.

4. Add fruit and cream to milk mixture and refrigerate until cold. Garnish with fruit or mint.

Makes about 12 cups.

Hot Mulled Wine

3 cups **sugar**
1 teaspoon dried **lemon peel**
1 teaspoon dried **orange peel**
2 **cloves**
1 stick **cinnamon**
2 cups **water**
1 (64-ounce) bottle **red wine**
1/2 cup **Madeira or sherry**

1. In a 3-quart container, combine all ingredients except wine and Madeira. Stir to dissolve sugar. Cook 5 minutes, uncovered.

2. Add wine and cook 5 minutes, uncovered; rest 5 minutes. Repeat until drink has cooked 30 minutes.

3. Add Madeira; let stand until ready to serve.

Makes about 16 cups.

Orange Tea Punch

1 (9-ounce) jar **Tang**
1/2 (6 1/2-ounce) package **lemonade mix**
3/4 cup **sugar** or more to taste
1-1/4 cups **instant tea**
1 teaspoon **cinnamon**
3/4 teaspoon **ginger**
1 teaspoon **cloves,** ground
1/4 teaspoon **nutmeg**

In a bowl, combine all ingredients. Store in an airtight 1-quart container.

Makes 64 servings.

One Cup

1-2 teaspoons **tea mix**
1 cup hot **water**

In a cup, add water to mix. Cook 2 minutes, uncovered.

Rompope

1 quart **half and half**
2-1/4 cups **sugar**
1 **vanilla pod** or 1 tablespoon **vanilla extract**
10 **egg yolks,** beaten
1 cup **vodka**

1. In a 2-quart container, cook half and half 5 minutes, uncovered.
2. Cool. Add sugar and vanilla pod or extract. Stir to dissolve sugar. Cook 10 minutes, uncovered. Stir every 2 minutes.
3. Cool. Slowly add egg yolks. Beat continually. For best results, use electric mixer or blender.
4. Add vodka slowly.
5. Cover until bubbles have disappeared.
6. Strain and bottle. Keep refrigerated.

Makes about 9 cups.

Spiced V8 Juice

1 (46-ounce) can **V8 juice**
3/4 cup **celery** tops
2 **beef bouillon cubes**
1 teaspoon **celery salt**
1 **bay leaf**
2 teaspoons **sugar**
Salt and **pepper** to taste
4 drops **Tabasco sauce**
1 teaspoon **beef tea**
1 tablespoon dried **parsley flakes**
3 tablespoons **lemon juice**
1 **lemon,** sliced thin

1. Into a 1-quart container, pour 2 cups V8 juice. Add the remaining ingredients except rest of V8 juice and thinly sliced lemon; stir. Cook 6 minutes, uncovered. Stir every 30 seconds. Let stand 4 minutes.

2. Pour the remaining V8 juice into a pitcher or jar. Strain the seasoned juice into this remaining juice.

3. Refrigerate; serve when cold. Garnish with lemon slices.

Makes 6-8 cups.

APPETIZERS

"I took the hot cakes, how could I help it? . . . and dipped them in a sauce, and then I ate them," said the ancient Greek writer, Athenaeus. He certainly had a craving for appetizers, and do I know how he felt! Are you guilty of just one last dip? Most of us are.

You can serve appetizers before meals or as the main attraction at parties. Remember, when served before a meal, they should be light; complement and contrast them with your menu. The present-day custom of serving appetizers with drinks before a meal probably originated in Russia. The *Zakuski*, or the mini-meal before the main course, was served in a room adjoining the dining room and consisted of many varieties of foods that were washed down with wine and liquor. The habit of eating before a meal to pique the appetite spread into many countries centuries ago.

Appetizers, both hot and cold, are presented in this book. Prepare hot appetizers the day ahead, refrigerate, and then reheat on paper towels or in a basket just before serving. If you own a portable cart, you can wheel the kitchen to the guests and both entertain and cook at the same time.

Since the recipes are created for speed as well as taste, last-minute preparation is possible. I had to make use of this convenience when several Arabian students came for a potluck dinner and the family in charge of the main dish was late arriving. The students spoke broken English and we spoke no Arabic. The original appetizers and dip disappeared; silence captured the room. What was I to do? I worried, waited, and watched the clock. Finally, I decided to prepare more appetizers. As I cooked in the kitchen, my son Kent took the students on a tour through the house.

I first knew what he was up to when he walked into the kitchen, followed by the students. He turned the garbage disposal on and off, opened some cabinet doors, and took out an electric mixer and waffle iron. The appliances survived a thorough examination, but my microwave oven was the highlight of the tour. The students pitched in and not only helped me make the appetizers, but also watched them cook. After that, everyone felt at home while we waited for the tardy casserole.

Appetizer Convenience Foods Guide

Place all appetizers in a circular or spoke pattern. Cook 6 at a time on a paper towel, uncovered.

Frozen

NAME	AMOUNT	TIME (FROZEN)
Beef Taquitos	11-1/2 oz. (6)	4-5 min.
Cocktail Tacos	5-1/2 oz.	1 min. 10 sec.
Egg Rolls	6 oz. (12)	1 min. 10 sec.
Mixed Appetizers, Precooked	(6)	1 min. 10 sec.
Pizza Snack Tray	7-1/4 oz. (15)	1 min. 10 sec.

Nut Roasting Guide

NAME	AMOUNT	DIRECTIONS	TIME
Almonds, Whole or Slivered	1/2 cup	Spread nuts in single layer in shallow container. Stir every 60 sec.	6-8 min., uncovered, or until golden.
Cashews, Raw	1 cup	Spread nuts in single layer in shallow container. Stir every 60 sec.	10-12 min.

NAME	AMOUNT	DIRECTIONS	TIME
		Pour 1 teaspoon vegetable oil evenly over the nuts. Sprinkle with salt. Stir to coat.	
Chestnuts, Raw	1-1/2 to 2 dozen	Cut crisscross slashes in each nut. Spread nuts in single layer in shallow container. Stir. After cool, peel off shell.	1 min., uncovered, or until nuts are soft when squeezed. Stand 5 min.
Peanuts, Raw, Blanched or Unblanched	1 cup	Spread nuts in single layer in shallow container. Stir every 60 sec. Pour 1 teaspoon vegetable oil evenly over nuts. Sprinkle with salt. Stir to coat.	6-8 min., uncovered.
Pine Nuts	1/2 cup	Spread nuts in single layer in shallow container. Stir every 60 sec.	6-8 min., uncovered, or until golden.
Pumpkin Seeds	1 cup	Rinse fibers from seeds. Sprinkle light coating of salt in the bottom of shallow container. Spread damp seeds in single layer on the salt. Stir every 60 sec.	6-7 min., uncovered, or until seeds are crisp.
Sunflower Seeds, Hulled	1 cup	Rinse fibers from seeds. Sprinkle light coating of salt in bottom of shallow container. Spread damp seeds in single layer on the salt. Stir every 60 sec.	5 min., uncovered, or until crisp.

NAME	AMOUNT	DIRECTIONS	TIME
Winter Squash Seeds	1 cup	Rinse fibers from seeds. Sprinkle light coating of salt in bottom of shallow container. Spread damp seeds in single layer on the salt. Stir every 60 sec.	6-7 min., uncovered, or until crisp.

Artichoke Squares

2 (6-ounce) jars marinated **artichoke hearts**, drained
4 **eggs**, beaten
3 tablespoons instant **minced onion**
1 teaspoon **garlic salt**
1/4 cup **bread crumbs**
1/4 teaspoon **salt**
1/8 teaspoon **pepper**
1/8 teaspoon **oregano**
1/8 teaspoon liquid **Tabasco sauce**
1-1/4 cups sharp **cheddar cheese**, grated
3 tablespoons dried **parsley flakes**

1. Chop artichokes and set aside.

2. In a bowl, combine eggs, onion, garlic salt, bread crumbs, and other seasonings except cheese and parsley flakes.

3. Pour into a greased shallow pan. Spoon chopped artichokes over the top.

4. Set filled container inside a larger container (with about 1 inch hot water).

5. Cook 6-7 minutes, uncovered. Rotate container 1/4 turn every 60 seconds.

6. Sprinkle cheese and parsley flakes over the top. Cook 1 minute, uncovered.

7. Cool and refrigerate. Cut in 1-inch squares. Serve cold or reheat for 3 minutes just before serving.

Makes about 12 squares.

Blue Cheese Cauliflower Hearts

1 (6/10-ounce) envelope **blue cheese salad dressing mix**
1 cup **sour cream**
2 (10-ounce) packages frozen **cauliflower hearts,** thawed, drained

1. In a 1-quart container, combine dressing mix and sour cream.
2. Add the cauliflower hearts; stir.
3. Cook 7-8 minutes, covered.
4. Serve hot with toothpicks.

Makes 8 servings.

Cartwheels

1/4 cup **mayonnaise**
6 slices **ham,** boiled
6 thin slices **turkey,** cooked
Salt and **pepper** to taste
1/4 teaspoon **garlic salt**
1-1/2 teaspoons dried **Italian seasoning**

1. Spread mayonnaise on each slice of meat.
2. Alternate ham and turkey slices in a long, overlapped, layered position. Sprinkle with seasoning.
3. Roll up and secure with toothpicks. Place on a flat container or wax paper, seam side down. Cook 4 minutes, loosely covered with wax paper.
4. Chill and cut each cartwheel in 5 individual pieces.

Makes 30 appetizers.

Clams in the Shell

24 **clams** in the shell
1/2 cup **butter,** melted
Tabasco sauce
Vinegar

1. Wash clams. In a 2-quart container, cook 6 clams at a time until shells open (see page 151). Take out as they open.

2. Rinse out sand.

3. Put about 1/2 teaspoon melted butter, 4 drops Tabasco sauce, and 1 or 2 drops vinegar in each shell.

4. Place on wax paper; cook, uncovered, 15 seconds.

Makes 24 appetizers.

Garlic Cereal Snack

1 (12-ounce) box **Rice Chex**
1 (1-pound 6-ounce) box **Wheat Chex**
1 (10-ounce) box **Cheerios**
1 (9-ounce) box **pretzels**
5 cups **mixed nuts**
3/4 cup **butter**
1-1/2 teaspoons **garlic salt**
1 teaspoon **onion salt**
1 teaspoon **salt**

1. In a 4-quart container, combine cereals, pretzels, and nuts.

2. In a cup, cook butter 2 minutes, uncovered, or until melted. Add salts; stir.

3. Pour sauce over cereal mixture; stir to coat evenly. Cook 9-11 minutes, uncovered. Stir every 2 minutes.

Makes about 13 cups.

Stuffed Clams

20 **clams or oysters** in the shell
4 slices **bacon**
1 (4-ounce) can **mushrooms**, chopped
1 tablespoon dried **parsley flakes**
1 cup fine **bread crumbs**
1/3 cup **butter**, melted
Salt and **pepper** to taste

1. Wash clams. In a 2-quart container, cook 6 clams at a time until shells open (see page 151). Take out as they open.

2. Remove clams from shells, rinse, and chop. Rinse shells.

3. Cook bacon. See guide (page 92).

4. In a bowl, combine all the ingredients.

5. Put a small portion of the mixture into each shell. Place on a paper towel. Cook 15 seconds, loosely covered with wax paper. Brown in microwave oven with browning element or brown conventionally.

Makes 20 appetizers.

NOTE: Large clams need additional bread crumbs and time.

Crab Fondue

1 (6 1/2-ounce) can **crab meat**
1 (10 1/2-ounce) can **cream of chicken soup**
1 (8-ounce) package **cream cheese**
2 tablespoons instant **minced onion**
1/4 teaspoon **curry powder**

1. In a 1 1/2-quart container, combine all the ingredients; stir.

2. Cook 6 minutes, covered. Stir every 60 seconds.

3. To serve, place in fondue pot or chafing dish. Dip with crackers or French bread.

Island Wrap-ups

8 chicken livers
1 (8-ounce) can **water chestnuts**
8 slices **bacon**

1. Cut each ingredient in half.

2. Place water chestnut on a piece of liver and wrap with bacon. Fasten securely with toothpick.

3. Place on a paper towel; cook 5-6 minutes, loosely covered with paper towels. Turn twice.

Makes 16 appetizers

NOTE: A date or pineapple chunk can be substituted for the water chestnut.

Stuffed Grape Leaves

1 cup **rice,** uncooked
1-1/2 pounds ground **lamb**
1 teaspoon ground **cinnamon**
2 teaspoons ground **cardamom**
1 (12-ounce) jar **grape leaves,** rinsed
1 teaspoon **olive oil**
4 teaspoons **garlic powder**
1 (1-pound 13-ounce) can **tomato puree**
1/2 cup **water**
Salt and **pepper** to taste

1. Cook rice. See guide (page 134).

2. In a bowl, combine rice, lamb, cinnamon, and cardamom.

3. Place a small portion of mixture on each grape leaf. Roll up from bottom of leaf; fold in sides.

4. In a 3-quart container greased with olive oil, layer 1/2 of stuffed grape leaves seam side down.

5. In a bowl, combine garlic powder, tomato puree, water, salt, and pepper.

6. Pour 1/2 of sauce over stuffed grape leaves.

7. Cook 12-15 minutes, covered. Serve in sauce with toothpicks.

Makes 50-55 appetizers.

Tortilla Chip Meatballs

1 pound **ground beef**
1 (4 3/4-ounce) can **liver spread**
1-1/2 teaspoons **prepared mustard**
Salt and **pepper** to taste
1/2 cup fine **bread crumbs**
3 tablespoons dried **parsley flakes**
2 **eggs**, beaten
2 cups cheese-flavored **tortilla chips**, crushed

1. In a bowl, combine all ingredients except chips.

2. Shape into 1-inch balls. Refrigerate 8 hours or overnight.

3. Before cooking, roll meatballs in the crushed tortilla chips.

4. Place on paper towel. Cook 5-6 minutes, uncovered. Turn every 2 minutes. Let stand 5 minutes, loosely covered.

Makes about 30-35 appetizers.

Mushroom Snails

24 large **mushroom caps**
1 (4 1/2-ounce) can **snails** (about 24)
1 tablespoon **garlic powder**
1/2 cup **butter**

1. Clean mushrooms. Break off stems; pat dry.

2. Place 1 snail in each mushroom cap.

3. In a cup, combine butter and garlic. Cook 1 minute, uncovered. Stir.

4. Dip each snail-filled mushroom into the garlic butter. Place on wax paper.

5. Cook 1-2 minutes, loosely covered with wax paper. Baste with garlic butter once.

Makes 24 appetizers.

NOTE: When cooking snails in shells, use above cooking time.

Stuffed Mushrooms

20 large fresh **mushrooms**
3 tablespoons **butter**
1 cup fine **bread crumbs**
3/4 cup canned **grated Parmesan cheese**
2 tablespoons instant **minced onion**
1/2 teaspoon **salted sunflower seeds**
1-1/2 tablespoons dried **parsley flakes**
1/2 tablespoon **pepper** (fresh ground)
1/2 teaspoon **seasoned salt**
1/2 cup **vermouth**
1 tablespoon **lemon juice**
1/2 cup **cheddar cheese,** cut in small cubes

1. Wash mushrooms; break off stems; pat dry; mince stems.

2. In a 1-quart container, cook butter 10 seconds, uncovered, or until melted.

3. Add remaining ingredients except cheddar cheese, plus 1/4 cup minced mushroom stems; stir.

4. Put a small portion of the dressing mixture into the mushroom caps. Place in lightly buttered, shallow container. Cook 10 minutes, loosely covered with wax paper.

5. Place small piece of cheddar cheese on top of each mushroom. Cook 2-3 minutes, uncovered.

Makes 20 servings.

Sausage Puffs

2 cups **biscuit mix**
1 pound **hot sausage**
1 cup **cheddar cheese,** grated

1. In a bowl, combine all ingredients.

2. Form into 1-inch balls.

3. Place on paper towel.

4. Cook 7 minutes, loosely covered with a paper towel.

Makes about 30-32 puffs.

Shellfish Pinwheels

Dough

2 sticks **pie dough mix**
3/4 teaspoon **prepared mustard**
2-3 tablespoons boiling hot
clam tomato juice
1 cup **seafood cocktail sauce**

1. In a bowl, make pie dough according to package directions except add mustard and replace water with hot clam tomato juice which has been cooked 30 seconds, uncovered.

2. Roll out dough in a 15 x 6-inch rectangle on a lightly floured breadboard.

3. Spread filling evenly over the dough.

4. Roll up jelly-roll style and cut in 1-inch slices.

5. Place on a greased, flat container. Cook 12 pinwheels at a time 14-15 minutes, until crust is slightly dry to the touch. Rotate 1/4 turn every 60 seconds.

6. Serve with cocktail sauce for dips.

Filling

1 (6 1/2-ounce) can **crab meat,**
drained, flaked
1/3 cup **celery,** minced
1/4 cup **mayonnaise**
1 tablespoon dried **parsley**
flakes

In a bowl, combine all ingredients.

Makes about 15 appetizers.

Hot Herbed Shrimp

1-1/4 tablespoons **whole allspice**
1 teaspoon **salt**
1 tablespoon **whole cloves**
1/2 teaspoon **Tabasco sauce**
3 **bay leaves**
4 **garlic cloves**
2 **lemons,** sliced
3 tablespoons instant **minced onion**
2-1/2 quarts **water**
2 pounds **shrimp,** raw, unpeeled
1 cup **butter or seafood sauce**

1. In a large container, place all ingredients except washed shrimp and butter. Cook 10 minutes, uncovered. Stand 10 minutes; cook 10 minutes.

2. Let shrimp marinate in the hot liquid mixture for 10 minutes, covered; drain.

3. Cook butter 3 minutes, uncovered.

4. Serve shrimp hot with melted butter, or chill and serve with a seafood sauce.

Makes about 8 servings.

NOTE: 1 packet of Shrimp Sauce and Crab Boil may be substituted for first eight ingredients.

SALADS

"Salad freshens without enfeebling and fortifies without irritating," mused French chef Brillat-Savarin. That is so, if we do not eat in excess. When they are served as the first course, we are often tempted to overindulge in eating salads—we should not eat them as if we were Apicius, the belly-god.

I often follow the custom of serving salads as an entree for a luncheon or light supper. Most of us couldn't do without them. It seems strange now that only two hundred years ago they were not even included in recipe books. Subsequently, salads became so popular that Sydney Smith, in a burst of gratitude, wrote the poem, "A Recipe for Salads," in which he exclaimed:

To make this condiment your poet begs
The pounded yellow of two hard-boiled eggs;
Two boiled potatoes, passed through kitchen sieve.
Smoothness and softness to the salad give;
Let onion atoms lurk within the bowl,
And half suspected animate the whole;
Of mordant mustard add a single spoon,
Distrust the condiment that bites so soon;
But deem it not, thou man of herbs, a fault
To add a double quantity of salt;
Four times the spoon with oil from Lucca crown,
And twice with vinegar, procured from town;
And lastly, o'er the flavored compound toss
A magic soupçon of anchovy sauce.
O green and glorious! O herbaceous treat!

'T would tempt the dying anchorite to eat;
Back to the world he'd turn his fleeting soul,
And plunge his fingers in the salad-bowl;
Serenely full, the epicure would say,
"Fate cannot harm me,—I have dined to-day."

SYDNEY SMITH

Salads, the dishes compiled of any number of vegetables, herbs, eggs, fish, shellfish, poultry, meats, and seasonings, may be served hot, cold, or at room temperature—with your imagination as the only limit. Remember, any dried or starchy vegetable seasons best while hot, so always season immediately after cooking.

Some of the salads in this book can be prepared entirely in the microwave oven; other recipes call for only part of the ingredients to be cooked. Let the microwaves dissolve gelatin, soften cheese, fry bacon, and heat oil-and-vinegar-base salad dressings for you.

Several hot salad recipes are listed and can be served with the same approval traditionally given to their cold, crisp, green relatives. Most hot salads contain a built-in plus: when prepared the day ahead and refrigerated, they can be reheated minutes before serving to save a last-minute rush.

I have not included many gelatin-mold salads because I feel they are easier to make the conventional way. Information on page 33 will help you use gelatin in your own recipes.

Salads: Points to Remember

1. Hot salads can be easily cooked in the microwave oven.
2. Reheat hot salads if they become cool for two to three minutes before serving.
3. Reheat hot salads that have been refrigerated. Add three to four minutes cooking time.
4. Use the microwave oven to prepare parts of some salads: cook bacon; cook dressings; heat dressings; heat water for gelatin; and cook vegetables or fruits.

Gelatins: Points to Remember

1. Place flavored three-ounce gelatin in a one-quart measure; add one cup water; stir. Cook two minutes, uncovered. Stir twice during cooking time. Add one cup cold water.
2. Dissolve unflavored gelatin in cold water or other liquid first, then heat to dissolve completely.
3. If gelatin mixture becomes cool, reheat until proper consistency.
4. Cool gelatin before folding into whipped cream or egg whites.

Hot Curry Chicken Salad

1 chicken, cooked, diced
3/4 cup **chutney**
2 tablespoons **curry powder**
1/2 cup **mayonnaise**
1 cup **toasted almonds**
1 cup **celery**, chopped

In a 2-quart container, combine all ingredients. Cook 8-9 minutes, covered. Stir 3 times.

Makes 4-6 servings.

Jellied Corned Beef Salad

1 (3-ounce) package **lemon jello**
1 (10 1/2-ounce) can **consommé**
1 **onion**, grated
1 (2 1/2-ounce) can **corned beef**
1 cup **celery**, diced
4 **eggs**, hard cooked, shelled, sliced
2 tablespoons **lemon juice**
1 teaspoon **Worcestershire sauce**
Mayonnaise

1. In a 1/2-quart container, combine jello and 1 cup consommé. Cook 2 minutes, uncovered. Stir every 30 seconds.

2. Add remaining consommé; stir. Set aside.

3. In a large bowl, combine remaining ingredients except mayonnaise. Add jello mixture; stir.

4. Grease 1 1/2-quart mold with mayonnaise. Pour jello into mold and chill.

Makes 6-8 servings.

Iman Baaldi Eggplant Salad

1 large **eggplant**
1 (15-ounce) can **stewed tomatoes,** drained
4 tablespoons instant **minced onion**
1/2 cup **currant jelly**
1/8 teaspoon **thyme**
1 teaspoon **olive oil**
2 **bay leaves**

1. Pierce eggplant with a fork and cook on wax paper for 8-10 minutes. Remove from oven while still slightly firm.

2. Cut in half lengthwise. Scrape out pulp.

3. In a 1 1/2-quart container, combine tomatoes, onion, currant jelly, and eggplant pulp. Cook 4-5 minutes, covered.

4. Fill eggplant halves with mixture. Sprinkle with thyme and pour oil over the top. Place a bay leaf on each.

5. Cook on a paper towel for 3 minutes, loosely covered with wax paper.

6. Cool and refrigerate. Serve cold.

Makes 2-4 servings.

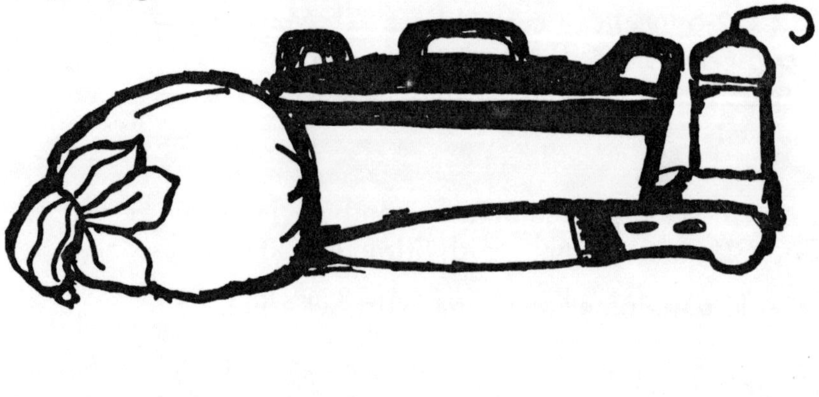

Layered Lettuce

1 head **lettuce**
5 slices **bacon,** cut in
5 sections
3 **eggs,** hard cooked, chopped
1 cup **onions,** chopped
1 (10-ounce) package frozen
chopped potatoes, thawed
3 tablespoons **bacon grease**
1/3 cup **vinegar**
1 teaspoon **salt**
1 tablespoon **sugar**

1. Soak lettuce leaves 1/2 hour in cold water.

2. In a rectangular container, cook bacon 3 minutes, loosely covered with a paper towel. Stir every 30 seconds. Remove bacon with slotted spoon; crumble.

3. In a bowl, alternate layers of lettuce, crumbled bacon, eggs, onions, and potatoes.

4. In a 1-quart measure, stir bacon grease and remaining ingredients. Cook 1 minute 30 seconds to 2 minutes, uncovered. Stir after first 30 seconds. Pour over layered ingredients. Cook 2 minutes, covered.

Makes 6-8 servings.

Hot German Potato Salad

4 medium **potatoes, peeled,**
sliced
4 slices **bacon,** cut in
5 sections
1 **onion,** diced
2-1/2 tablespoons **sugar**
2 tablespoons **flour**
1 **beef bouillon cube**
1 teaspoon **dry mustard**
3/4 teaspoon **salt**
3/4 teaspoon **celery seeds**
1/8 teaspoon **pepper**
3 tablespoons dried **parsley**
flakes
4 tablespoons **bacon grease**
1/4 cup **vinegar**
1/2 cup **water**

1. Cook potatoes. See guide (page 162).

2. In a 2-quart container, cook bacon and onion 3 minutes, loosely covered with a paper towel. Stir every 30 seconds. Remove with a slotted spoon; set aside.

3. In a 1-quart glass measure, add sugar, flour, beef bouillon cube, mustard, salt, celery seeds, pepper, and parsley to warm, but not hot, bacon grease; stir. Cook 1 minute, uncovered. Stir after first 30 seconds.

4. Add vinegar and water and cook 1 minute 30 seconds to 2 minutes, uncovered. Stir twice.

5. Add cut up potatoes and crumbled bacon. Mix. Let stand 4 minutes, covered.

Makes 4-6 servings.

Hot Pea-Potato Salad

1 (12-ounce) package frozen **hash brown potatoes**
1 (10-ounce) package frozen **peas**, defrosted
1 (2-ounce) jar sliced **pimentos**, drained
1 cup **mayonnaise**
1/3 cup **French dressing**
1/2 cup **sour cream**
3 tablespoons dried **parsley flakes**
Salt and **pepper** to taste
1/2 teaspoon **paprika**

1. Cook potatoes in package 4 minutes; turn once.

2. In a greased, 2-quart container, combine all ingredients except paprika; stir. Sprinkle with paprika.

3. Cook 10-12 minutes, covered. Serve hot.

Makes 4-6 servings.

Macaroni-Tuna Salad

1 cup **macaroni**
1 (7-ounce) can **tuna**
4 cups **cabbage**, shredded
1/4 cup **sweet pickles**, chopped
1 (2-ounce) can **chopped pimentos**
Salt and **pepper** to taste
1/2 teaspoon **celery salt**
1-1/2 teaspoons **sugar**
3 tablespoons **vegetable oil**
1 tablespoon instant **minced onion**
3 tablespoons **lemon juice**
1/2 cup **canned milk**

1. Cook macaroni. See guide (page 118). Drain and rinse.

2. In a large bowl, add remaining ingredients to macaroni; mix.

3. Serve warm, or refrigerate and serve cold.

Makes 4-6 servings.

Creole Shrimp Salad

1 cup uncooked **rice**
2 tablespoons dried **sweet pepper flakes**
1 cup **cauliflower**, diced
1-1/2 tablespoons instant **minced onion**
1 (2 1/4-ounce) can **ripe olives**, chopped
1/3 cup **mayonnaise**
3 tablespoons **lemon juice**
5 tablespoons **cream-style French dressing**
Salt and **pepper** to taste
1 cup **shrimp**, precooked, cleaned

1. Cook rice according to guide except cook 5 minutes less. See guide (page 134).

2. In a 1 1/2-quart container, combine remaining ingredients except shrimp.

3. Add rice; stir.

4. Cook 7 minutes, covered. Stir 3 times.

5. Mix in shrimp. Cook 1 minute, covered. Let stand 3 minutes, covered.

6. Serve hot, or refrigerate and serve cold.

Makes 4 servings.

Hot Slaw

6 strips **bacon,** cut in
5 sections each
1/2 teaspoon **celery salt**
1/4 cup **brown sugar**
1/2 teaspoon **dry mustard**
1/4 cup **vinegar**
1/2 teaspoon **salt**
4 tablespoons **bacon grease**
1 medium **cabbage,** shredded
1/2 cup **peanuts**

1. In a 2-quart container, cook bacon 3 minutes, loosely covered with a paper towel. Remove with slotted spoon; crumble; set aside.

2. In a 1-quart glass measure, add remaining ingredients except cabbage and peanuts to bacon grease; stir. Cook 1 minute, uncovered. Stir after 30 seconds.

3. In a 1-quart container, place cabbage, crumbled bacon, and peanuts; stir. Pour hot dressing over salad; stir. Cook 1 minute, covered.

Makes 6 to 8 servings.

Wilted Lettuce or Spinach

2 heads **lettuce or endive** or
2 bunches **spinach,** washed,
broken into pieces
1/3 **onion,** minced
6 slices **bacon,** cut in
5 sections
1/4 cup **wine vinegar**
1-1/2 tablespoons **sugar**
1 tablespoon **water**
3 tablespoons **bacon grease**
Salt and **pepper** to taste
2 **eggs,** hard cooked, chopped
(optional)

1. In a large bowl, place torn lettuce, endive, or spinach and sprinkle with minced onion.

2. In a 2-quart container, cook bacon 3 minutes, loosely covered with a paper towel. Stir every 30 seconds. Remove bacon with a slotted spoon; crumble; set aside.

3. In a 1-quart glass measure, add wine vinegar, sugar, and water to slightly cooled bacon grease. Cook 1 minute, uncovered.

4. Pour immediately over spinach or lettuce. Salt and pepper to taste. Add crumbled bacon and chopped eggs.

Makes 8-10 servings.

NOTE: Salad can be made up to step 4 several hours before serving. Just before serving, reheat bacon grease-vinegar-sugar dressing for 1 minute, uncovered.

Tostada Salad

1 pound **ground beef**
1 cup **onions,** chopped
1 (15-ounce) can **red kidney beans,** drained
1 (1 1/4-ounce) envelope **taco seasoning mix**
1/4 teaspoon **salt**
1 head **lettuce,** cut in pieces
2 cups **cheddar cheese,** grated
1 cup **Thousand Island** or **Catalina** dressing
1 (9-ounce) package **taco chips**
2 large **avocados,** sliced
6 **tomatoes,** cut in wedges

1. In a 2-quart container, sauté meat and onions. Cook 5 minutes, uncovered. Stir every 30 seconds.

2. Add red kidney beans, taco seasoning mix, and salt. Cook 5 minutes, covered.

3. In a salad bowl, combine the remaining ingredients; reserve 1 cup chips. Add beef mixture; toss lightly.

4. Garnish with reserved chips.

Makes 6-8 servings.

Burgundy Wine Mold

1 cup **water**
1 (6-ounce) package **raspberry-flavored gelatin**
1 (16-ounce) can **whole berry cranberry sauce**
1/2 cup **Burgundy**
1 (8-ounce) can **crushed pineapple**
1/2 cup **walnuts,** chopped
2 (11-ounce) cans **mandarin oranges**
1/2 cup **celery,** chopped

1. In a 2-quart container, heat water 2 minutes, uncovered. Add gelatin; stir.

2. Add whole berry cranberry sauce. Cook 3 minutes 30 seconds, uncovered. Stir every 30 seconds.

3. Add remaining ingredients; stir. Pour into a 1 1/2-quart mold. Refrigerate until firm. Add topping before serving.

Topping

1 (8-ounce) package **cream cheese**
2 cups **commercial dessert topping**
1/2 teaspoon dried **orange peel** or 1 teaspoon fresh **orange peel**

Blend cream cheese and dessert topping until smooth. Mix in orange peel.

Makes 6-8 servings.

NOTE: For best results, use fresh orange peel.

SAUCES & SOUPS

Escoffier commanded cooks: "Devote yourself to your sauce, for a sauce emphasizes flavors, provides contrast, makes perfection complete." Sauces perk up the most ordinary food. Keep plenty of canned white sauce on hand, as it is the basis of many other sauces and the one thing you can't do without. After you season and add your own personal touch, no one will ever guess your sauce came from a can.

Perhaps the first sauce originated was the vinaigrette: one-third vinegar, two-thirds oil, with salt and seasonings to taste. We misnamed it French Dressing—much of the world was using it before France was a nation. The French now boast of over two hundred different liquid seasonings for food. The United States, a melting pot of people, assimilates countless sauces from many nations of the world.

Soups emphasize the blending of flavors. The aroma of piping hot pottage can be very tempting, as Esau found when he sold his birthright for some lentil soup. I'm sure we wouldn't go that far—or would we? Sometimes soup smells enticing. . . .

Today, canned soups substitute for, or are the basis of, many good sauces; and canned soups lend themselves to elegance with just a little help from the cook. For instance, add a touch of sour cream, wine, brandy, or sherry to your soups instead of water. Presto!—a new personality surfaces. Be even more creative: top soup with fresh or frozen chives, thin cucumber slices, croutons, grated cheese, or whatever you have on hand that complements the soup—or try, as I have, to mix various soup flavors together to achieve a brand new twist.

A canned soup, doubling as a sauce, saved the day for me. Immediately before serving lunch to friends, disaster struck. My large pancake roll stuck to the waxed paper. Quickly, I peeled off the pancake, in pieces, and mixed them with the stuffing in a large casserole. It looked absolutely horrible. What to do? I then covered the whole "mess" with beer-flavored shrimp soup. The microwave oven not only cooked my sauce fast, but also saved my pride.

When making your own soup, don't skimp on ingredients, because it may turn into the calamity described by Abraham Lincoln as a soup "that was made by boiling the shadow of a pigeon that had starved to death."

Sauces: Points to Remember

1. Most sauces can be cooked in a four-cup (one-quart) glass measuring cup, uncovered.
2. Stir often with a wooden spoon, which can be left in sauce during cooking period.
3. When flour and cornstarch are used as the thickening agent, the sauce should boil to prevent lumps.
4. When eggs or egg yolks are used to thicken, the sauce should not boil.

Sauce Convenience Foods Guide

Boxed

NAME	AMOUNT	DIRECTIONS	TIME
Gravy Mix	1 env.	In a 1/2-qt. container, prepare according to pkg. directions; stir. Stir after first 60 sec.	2 min. to 2 min. 30 sec., uncovered.
Cheese, Hollandaise, Sour Cream, or White Sauce	1 env.	In a 1/2-qt. container, prepare according to pkg. directions; stir. Stir after first 60 sec.	2 min. 30 sec. to 3 min., uncovered.

Canned

NAME	AMOUNT	DIRECTIONS	TIME
Sauce	10-1/2-oz.	Pour into a 1/2-qt. container. Stir once after first 2 min.	4 min., uncovered.

Frozen

NAME	AMOUNT	DIRECTIONS	TIME
Sauce	8 oz.	Remove from carton. Defrost pouch.	2 min.
		Slit pouch and pour into 1/2-qt. container. Stir once after first 60 sec. Stir before using.	3 min. 30 sec., uncovered.

Barbecue Sauce

1 (20-ounce) bottle **catsup**
10 ounces **water**
1 cup **sugar**
1 or 2 teaspoons **pepper**
1 teaspoon **liquid smoke** (optional)

1. In a 2-quart container, combine all ingredients; blend until sugar dissolves.

2. Cook 8 minutes, uncovered. Stir every 30 seconds. Sauce should be thick.

Makes about 5-1/2 cups.

Cheese Sauce

2-1/2 tablespoons **butter,** melted
2 tablespoons **flour**
1/4 teaspoon **dry mustard**
1 cup **milk** or 1/2 cup **milk** and 1/2 cup **beer**
1 cup sharp **cheddar cheese,** grated
Salt and **pepper**

1. In a 1-quart container, combine butter, flour, and dry mustard; blend until smooth.

2. Gradually add milk, stirring constantly. Cook 1 minute, uncovered.

3. Gradually add cheese; blend until smooth.

4. Cook 3 or 4 minutes, covered. Stir every 30 seconds.

5. Salt and pepper to taste.

Makes about 2 cups.

Super Quick Cheese Sauce

1 (10 1/2-ounce) can **cheddar cheese soup**
1/4 cup **milk** or 1/3 cup **beer**
Salt and **pepper** to taste

1. In a 1-quart container, combine all ingredients; blend until smooth.

2. Cook 3 minutes, uncovered. Stir every 30 seconds.

Makes about 1-3/4 cups.

NOTE: The beer in the sauce is a taste treat. Add a can of mushrooms to make Mushroom Cheese Sauce.

Hot Chili Sauce

1 (10-ounce) can Spanish brand **tomato sauce**
1 (15-ounce) can regular **tomato sauce**
1 (7-ounce) can **green chilies**, chopped
1/8 teaspoon **oregano**
1/4 teaspoon **garlic**
Salt and **pepper** to taste

1. In a 1-quart container, combine all ingredients; blend until smooth.

2. Cook 6 minutes, uncovered. Stir every 60 seconds.

Makes about 3 cups.

Hot Horseradish Sauce

1 cup fine **bread crumbs**
1/3 cup **milk**
2 tablespoons **horseradish sauce**
1-1/2 tablespoons **sugar**
1-1/2 cups **cream**
1 teaspoon **vinegar**
Salt to taste

1. In a 1-quart container, moisten bread crumbs in milk for 1 minute. Cook 30 seconds, covered.

2. Add remaining ingredients; stir to blend. Cook 3 minutes, uncovered. Stir every 30 seconds.

Makes about 2-1/4 cups.

Quick Mornay Sauce

1 (10 1/2-ounce) can **cheddar cheese soup**
1 cup **cream**
1/8 teaspoon **cayenne**
1 **bay leaf**
1 tablespoon **sherry**
1 **egg yolk**

1. In a 1-quart container, combine all ingredients except sherry and egg yolk. Cook 3 minutes, uncovered. Stir twice.

2. Add sherry and egg yolk; stir. Cook 30 seconds, uncovered.

3. Remove bay leaf.

Makes about 2-1/2 cups.

NOTE: Spoon over food. Brown in microwave oven with browning element or conventionally.

Mustard Sauce

2 tablespoons **dry mustard**
1 tablespoon **flour**
1 cup **sugar**
1 cup **cream**
1/2 cup **vinegar**
1 **egg yolk**

1. In a 1-quart container, combine dry ingredients.
2. Add cream, vinegar, and egg yolk; stir until smooth.
3. Cook 4 minutes, uncovered. Stir every 30 seconds.

Makes about 2 cups.

Onion Soup Sauce

6 tablespoons **butter,** melted
3 tablespoons **flour**
1 (1-ounce) package **dried onion soup mix**
Salt and **pepper**
2-1/2 cups **milk** or 2 cups **milk** and 1/2 cup **sherry**
Salt and **pepper**

1. In a 1-quart container, combine butter, flour, and onion soup mix; blend until smooth.
2. Add salt and pepper to taste. Gradually add milk, stirring constantly.
3. Cook 3-4 minutes, uncovered. Stir every 30 seconds.

Makes about 2-3/4 cups.

Fast Shrimp Sauce

1 (10 1/2-ounce) can **shrimp soup**
1/2 teaspoon **cayenne**
1/2 cup **beer**
1 (2-ounce) jar **anchovies** (optional)

1. In a 1-quart container, combine all ingredients; blend until smooth.

2. Cook 4 minutes, covered. Stir every 30 seconds.

Makes about 2 cups.

Soy Sauce

1 cup **soy sauce**
1 teaspoon **powdered ginger**
2 tablespoons **green onion,** minced
1-1/4 teaspoons **garlic powder**
1 teaspoon **sesame oil** or **vegetable oil**
2-1/3 tablespoons **cider vinegar**
2 tablespoons **brown sugar**

1. In a 1/2-quart container, combine all ingredients; blend until smooth.

2. Cook 2 minutes, uncovered. Stir every 30 seconds.

Makes about 1-1/4 cups.

Tomato Catsup

3/4 cup **vinegar**
1/2 teaspoon **pickling spices**
2 pounds ripe **tomatoes,** chopped
1 medium **onion,** chopped
1 cup **apples,** peeled, cored, chopped
3/4 cup **sugar**
1/2 teaspoon **salt**
1/8 teaspoon **cayenne pepper**

1. In a 1-quart container, cook vinegar and pickling spice 1 minute 30 seconds, uncovered.

2. In a 2-quart container, combine tomatoes, onion, and apples. Cook 7 minutes, covered. Stir every 2 minutes.

3. Rub tomato mixture through a sieve or puree in blender (leave a little pulp behind).

4. In a 2-quart container, combine all ingredients; stir to dissolve sugar.

5. Cook 10 minutes, uncovered. Stir every 5 minutes.

6. Keep refrigerated.

Makes about 1-1/2 pints.

Sweet-Sour Sauce

1 tablespoon **vegetable oil**
4 tablespoons **cornstarch**
1/4 cup dried **sweet pepper flakes**
3/4 cup **sugar**
1/3 cup **catsup**
1 tablespoon **soy sauce**
1/2 cup **cider vinegar**
1/2 cup **pineapple chunks,** drained
Salt

1. In a 1-quart container, cook oil 15 seconds.

2. Stir in cornstarch; blend until smooth.

3. Add all ingredients except pineapple chunks and salt; stir. Cook 3 minutes, uncovered. Stir every 30 seconds.

4. Add pineapple chunks and cook 1 minute, uncovered.

5. Salt to taste.

Makes about 2 cups.

NOTE: There are many packaged and canned sweet-and-sour sauce products which may be substituted for this recipe.

Tomato Sauce

1 (15-ounce) can **tomato sauce**
3/4 tablespoon **butter**
4 tablespoons **lemon juice**
1 teaspoon **Worcestershire sauce**
1 teaspoon **sugar**
1 teaspoon **liquid smoke** or 1/2 teaspoon **Tabasco sauce**
Salt and **pepper** to taste

1. In a 1-quart container, combine all ingredients; blend until smooth.

2. Cook 4 minutes, uncovered. Stir every 30 seconds.

Makes about 1-3/4 cups.

White Sauce

5 tablespoons **butter**, melted
5 tablespoons **flour**
2 cups **milk**
1/4 teaspoon **cinnamon**
1/4 teaspoon **nutmeg**
Salt to taste
3 **egg yolks**, stirred (optional)

1. In a 1-quart container, blend butter and flour until smooth.
2. Gradually add milk; stir.
3. Cook 3 minutes, uncovered. Stir every 30 seconds.
4. Add remaining ingredients; blend. Cook 1 minute, uncovered.

Makes about 2-1/4 cups.

NOTE: For thicker sauce use 7-8 tablespoons butter and flour. For thinner sauce use 2 tablespoons butter and flour.

Other Sauces Made from White Sauce

1 (10 1/2-ounce) can **white sauce** or 1 recipe **white sauce** (page 49)

1. In a 1-quart container, stir white sauce and other ingredients until smooth.
2. Cook 2 minutes, uncovered. Stir. Continue to cook for 2 more minutes, uncovered.

Anchovy Sauce

1 (2-ounce) can chopped **anchovies** or 1-1/4 teaspoons **anchovy essence**

Add to white sauce.

Béchamel Sauce

1/4 cup **onion**
1/4 cup **carrot**
1/4 cup **celery**
1/4 cup **milk**

Puree in a blender; add to white sauce.

Caper Sauce

1 (3 1/2-ounce) jar **capers**, minced, with liquid
1 **bouillon cube**

Add to white sauce.

Cheese Sauce

1/2 cup **cheese**, grated
1/2 teaspoon **dry mustard**

Add to white sauce.

Cucumber Sauce

1 **cucumber**, peeled, chopped
1 teaspoon **lemon juice**
8 drops **green food coloring**
1/2 cup **cream**

Puree in a blender; add to white sauce.

Egg Sauce

4 **eggs**, hard cooked, peeled, minced
2 tablespoons dried **parsley flakes**
1/2 teaspoon **paprika**

Add to white sauce.

Fish Sauce

1 cup **fish stock**
4 tablespoons dried **parsley flakes**

Add to white sauce.

Hollandaise Sauce

1 **egg**, beaten
1 tablespoon **lemon juice**

Cook white sauce 3 minutes, uncovered. Whisk in egg and lemon juice; cook 1 minute, uncovered. Stir after 30 seconds.

Hot Horseradish Sauce

1 teaspoon **vinegar**
2 tablespoons **horseradish sauce**
1/2 teaspoon **sugar**

Add to white sauce.

Mustard Sauce

1 tablespoon **dry mustard**

Add to white sauce.

Onion Sauce

1/4 (1-ounce) envelope **dried onion soup**

Add to white sauce.

Oyster Sauce

1 (8-ounce) can **oysters,** minced, or 1 (8-ounce) can baby **oysters,** cut fine, and juice

Add to white sauce.

Parsley Sauce

4 tablespoons dried **parsley flakes**
1 teaspoon **lemon juice**

Add to white sauce.

Shrimp Sauce

1/2 pound **shrimp,** cooked
5 drops **red food coloring**
1 teaspoon **lemon juice**
1/4 cup **cream**
1/4 cup **celery,** diced (optional)

Puree in a blender; add to white sauce.

Tomato Sauce

1 (15-ounce) can **tomato puree**

In a glass measure, cook tomato puree 4 minutes, uncovered. Stir once. Cook white sauce the same way. Before serving, whisk together.

Soups: Points to Remember

1. Cook about two minutes for each cup of soup when using a combination precooked ingredient or reheating soup.
2. Cover soup when cooking.
3. Stir occasionally with a wooden spoon.
4. If convenient, cook soup several hours or the day before using. Reheat and serve.

Soup Convenience Foods Guide

Boxed

NAME	AMOUNT	DIRECTIONS	TIME
Dehydrated Soup Mix	1 env.	In a 1 1/2-qt. container, prepare according to pkg. directions. Stir once after first 2 min.	4-5 min., uncovered. Stand 5 min.

Canned

NAME	AMOUNT	DIRECTIONS	TIME
Soup	10-1/2 oz.	Pour soup into a 1 1/2-qt. container; stir. Stir once after first 2 min.	4-6 min., uncovered.

Frozen

NAME	AMOUNT	DIRECTIONS	TIME
Soup	8-oz. pouch	Defrost soup pouch.	2 min.
		Slit pouch and pour into a 1/2-qt. container. Stir once after first 60 sec. Stir before serving.	3 min. 30 sec. to 4 min.

Cold Spanish Avocado Soup

2 (13 3/4-ounce) cans **chicken broth**
1/2 cup instant **potato flakes**
2 teaspoons instant **minced onion**
1 (7-ounce) can **frozen avocado dip**, thawed
2 cups **cream**
1 (2-ounce) package dry **guacamole dip**
Salt and **pepper** to taste
1 (2 3/4-ounce) package **almonds**, slivered, toasted

1. In a 2-quart container, cook chicken broth 3 minutes, uncovered.

2. Add potato flakes and onion; beat with a fork to blend. Cook 4-5 minutes. Stir once.

3. Combine remaining ingredients except almonds. Blend until smooth.

4. Garnish with slivered almonds.

Makes 4-5 servings.

Creole Cheddar Cheese Soup

6 tablespoons instant **minced onion** or 1 medium (1 cup) **onion**, chopped
1/2 cup **green pepper**, chopped
1/4 teaspoon **cayenne pepper**
1/4 cup **bacon grease** or **butter**
1/2 cup **celery**, chopped
1/2 cup **dry white wine**
2 (10 1/2-ounce) cans **cheddar cheese soup**
1/2 cup frozen **chopped chives**
2 tablespoons **parsley flakes**
1 tablespoon **paprika**
Salt and **pepper** to taste

1. In a 2-quart container, cook onion, green pepper, and cayenne pepper in the bacon grease 3 minutes, lightly covered with wax paper. Stir every 30 seconds.

2. Add remaining ingredients; cook 7-9 minutes, covered.

Makes 3-4 servings.

Almond Chicken Soup

1 (10 1/2-ounce) can **cream of chicken soup**
2 cups **cream** or **half and half**
1/2 cup **milk**
2 tablespoons **butter,** melted
1/2 cup **onions,** chopped
1 **bay leaf**
1 cup **almonds,** blanched, finely ground
1/2 cup **almonds,** slivered

1. In a 2-quart container, combine all ingredients except slivered almonds. Blend until smooth.

2. Cook 9 minutes, covered. Stir every 2 minutes.

3. Garnish with slivered almonds.

Makes 3-4 servings.

NOTE: Grind the almonds in a hand grinder or in a blender.

Clam Chowder

6 slices **bacon,** cooked, crumbled
3 **green onions** and **tops,** chopped
5 medium **potatoes,** diced
2 tablespoons dried **sweet pepper flakes**
1/4 cup **celery** and **leaves,** chopped
1 **carrot,** chopped
1 teaspoon **garlic powder**
2 cups **water**
1 teaspoon **salt**
1/2 teaspoon **pepper**
1 teaspoon **Worcestershire sauce**
2 cups **clams with juice**
2 cups **cream**
6-8 drops **Tabasco sauce** or to taste

1. Cook bacon. See guide (page 92).

2. In a 3-quart container, combine all ingredients except clams, cream, and Tabasco.

3. Cook 12-14 minutes, covered, or until potatoes are done. Test with a fork.

4. In a container, cook clams with juice 3 minutes, covered. Add to hot vegetable mixture.

5. Pour in cream. Add Tabasco to taste; stir. Cook 5-7 minutes, covered. Stir twice.

Makes 6-8 servings.

Fast Goulash

2 cups **elbow macaroni**
1 pound **ground beef**
2 cups **onions**, chopped
2 tablespoons dried **sweet pepper flakes**
1 cup **celery**, chopped
1 tablespoon **paprika**
1/8 teaspoon **pepper**
1 teaspoon **garlic salt or powder**
1 (10 1/2-ounce) can **vegetable soup**
1 (6-ounce) can **tomato paste**
1 cup **water**
1 (15-ounce) can **kidney beans**, drained

1. Cook macaroni. See guide (page 118). Drain and rinse.

2. In a 3-quart container, cook meat, onions, pepper flakes, celery, and seasonings 4 minutes, loosely covered with wax paper. Stir every 60 seconds.

3. Add vegetable soup, tomato paste, water, kidney beans, and macaroni; stir. Cook 10-12 minutes, covered. Stir every 5 minutes.

Makes 6 servings.

Knockwurst and Sauerkraut Soup

4 slices **bacon**, cooked, crumbled
1 cup **onions**, minced
4 tablespoons **butter**
1 teaspoon **paprika**
1 (15-ounce) can **sauerkraut**
1 **bay leaf**
1 (10-ounce) package frozen **hash brown potatoes**, thawed
3 (10 1/2-ounce) cans **consommé**
4-6 **knockwurst**, peeled, sliced thin
1/2 cup **sour cream**

1. Cook bacon. See guide (page 92).

2. In a 2-quart container, cook onions in butter 3 minutes, uncovered. Stir every 30 seconds.

3. Add paprika, sauerkraut, bay leaf, and potatoes. Cook 6-7 minutes, covered. Stir every 2 minutes.

4. Add consommé, knockwurst, bacon, and sour cream; stir. Cook 9-11 minutes, covered. Stir twice.

Makes 6 servings.

Lobster Bisque

1 (10 1/2-ounce) can **tomato bisque soup**
1 (10 1/2-ounce) can **cream of mushroom soup**
1 (10 1/2-ounce) soup can **white wine**
1-1/2 cups **cream** or **half and half**
1 cup (or more) frozen **lobster,** cooked, flaked
2 tablespoons **butter**
1/2 teaspoon **nutmeg**
3 teaspoons dried **parsley flakes**

1. In a 2 1/2- or 3-quart container, combine all ingredients. Blend until smooth.

2. Cook 10-12 minutes, covered. Stir every 2 minutes.

Makes 4-6 servings.

Fast French Onion Soup

1/2 cup **butter,** melted
4 cups **dried bread,** large chunks (preferably French bread)
2 cups **onions,** chopped
2 (10 1/2-ounce) cans **onion soup**
2 cups **cheddar cheese,** grated

1. In a bowl, pour half of the butter over the bread chunks. Set aside.

2. In a 2-quart container, cook onions in the remaining butter 3 minutes, uncovered.

3. Add soup; cook 5 minutes, covered. Stir twice.

4. Place bread on top of soup and sprinkle with cheese. Brown in microwave oven with browning element or conventionally.

Makes 3-4 servings.

NOTE: The soup may be cooked in individual soup bowls or mugs.

Potato-Tuna Soup

8 slices **bacon**
2 tablespoons **butter,** melted
3 tablespoons instant **minced onion**
1 (5 1/2-ounce) package **scalloped potato mix** plus sauce
1 **bay leaf**
2-1/4 cups hot **water**
1-1/2 cups **milk**
1 (10 1/2-ounce) can **cream of chicken soup,** plus 1/2 can **water**
3 tablespoons dried **parsley flakes**
1 (12-ounce) can **Mexican-style corn,** undrained
1 (6 1/2-ounce) can **tuna**
1 (5 1/3-ounce) can **evaporated milk**
Salt and **pepper**

1. Cook bacon. See guide (page 92).

2. In a 3-quart container, cook onions in butter 30 seconds.

3. Add scalloped potatoes, sauce, bay leaf, water, milk, cream of chicken soup, water, and parsley flakes. Cook 8-10 minutes, covered. (Potatoes should be tender.) Stir every 2 minutes.

4. Stir in crumbled bacon, corn, tuna, and evaporated milk. Salt and pepper to taste. Cook 4-6 minutes, covered.

Makes 6-8 servings.

Vichyssoise

1 (10 3/4-ounce) can **cream of potato soup**
1 (10 1/2-ounce) can **cream of chicken soup**
1 (10 1/2-ounce) soup can **milk**
1 cup **half and half**
1/4 cup frozen **chopped chives**

1. In a 2 1/2- or 3-quart container, combine all ingredients except chives; beat until smooth.
2. Cook 8 minutes, covered. Stir once.
3. Refrigerate. Serve cold and garnish with chives.

Makes 3-4 servings.

MAIN DISHES

Many of our main dishes were first called "made dishes" by Archestratus, the ancient Greek writer who coined the phrase to mean all recipes composed of several ingredients. These dishes can be simple fare or the most complicated epicurean delights. According to Brillat-Savarin, in former times a dinner of importance began with oysters—and there were usually a good number of guests who didn't stop until they had gobbled a gross (12 dozen). Unfortunately, when guests drop by, we don't always have oysters on hand; but we should have convenience foods stored in the pantry.

Recently my microwave oven and fast recipes came in handy. On a Saturday night at about 7:30, two of our friends came to our house—carrying a bottle of wine. After greeting them, I asked my husband to join me in the kitchen.

The minute the door closed, he whispered, "What's going on?" A little louder, I answered, "I invited them. *Next* week. Not tonight." "You've got to be kidding," he replied. "No, I'm certain. They've mixed up the date. Look." I pointed to my kitchen calendar. "You'll have to eat again," I said, handing him some cheese and crackers on a tray. While he went back to our guests to play the grand host, I quickly opened a few cans, added some wine, and popped the "made dish" into the microwave oven. Three deep breaths later, I joined the guests.

Most of the main dishes in this book can be prepared under similar duress. Only, let's hope, not too many times!

You will find meats, fish, shellfish, sandwiches, pastas, rice, cheeses, and leftovers in this section. The recipes are all fast and simple to prepare when followed exactly as presented; but most gourmets believe that the best road to variety in cuisine is substitution, so feel free to experiment by using part or all convenience foods. Most of the meats and all of the shellfish can be interchanged. If you have a can of shrimp and no crab, by all means substitute; and add a little wine or beer instead of water or milk. Improvise or follow the directions exactly, for either way, you will create a time saver. Brillat-Savarin tells us, "The discovery of a new dish confers more happiness on mankind than the discovery of a new star"—so don't hesitate to experiment.

Cheeses: Points to Remember

1. Processed cheese melts smoother and can tolerate more cooking than natural cheese.
2. Don't overcook cheese because it will become stringy.

Cheese Croutons or Cheese Cookies

1/2 loaf of day-old **white or brown bread**, crusts cut off, cubed (1/2 inch)
4 tablespoons **butter**, melted
1 cup **cheddar cheese**, shredded, or **blue cheese**, crumbled

1. Dip bread cubes into butter and toss into cheese to coat.

2. Place croutons on a shallow buttered container or wax paper; cook 1 minute 30 seconds, uncovered. Stir every 30 seconds.

Makes about 2 cups croutons.

NOTE: To make cookies, use only cheddar cheese. Cut the bread with a cooky cutter or in squares. Cook the same as the croutons.

Cheese Loaf

2-1/2 cups fine **bread crumbs**
1 cup **milk**
1-1/2 cup **American or cheddar cheese,** grated
3 **eggs,** yolk and white beaten separately
1 (2-ounce) jar **pimentos,** chopped
1/8 teaspoon **salt**
2 tablespoons **dried sweet pepper flakes**
1 teaspoon **Worcestershire sauce**

1. In a large container, combine all ingredients except egg white; stir. Fold in beaten egg white. Pour into a buttered glass loaf pan.

2. Cook 7-9 minutes, uncovered.

Makes 6-8 servings.

Spinach Fettucini

1 pound medium or small **spinach noodles**
1/4 cup **vegetable oil**
1 teaspoon **garlic powder**
1 (10-ounce) package frozen **chopped spinach,** thawed, drained
1/2 (10 1/2-ounce) can **cream of chicken soup**
1/2 teaspoon dried **basil leaves**
4 tablespoons dried **parsley flakes**
1/2 cup canned **grated Parmesan cheese**
1 cup **ricotta cheese**
Salt and pepper
1 (2-ounce) can **pimentos,** diced

1. Cook noodles. See guide (page 118).

2. Pour oil into a 2-quart container. Sprinkle garlic in the oil and add spinach. Cook 2 minutes 30 seconds, uncovered. Stir every 30 seconds.

3. Add chicken soup, seasonings, and cheeses; stir. Cook 3 minutes, covered. Stir once.

4. Combine cheese-spinach mixture with the noodles. Salt and pepper to taste. Cook 3-4 minutes, covered. Garnish with pimento.

Makes 6-8 servings.

Fondue

1 pound **Gruyère** or **Dutch Gouda cheese**
4 drops **Tabasco sauce**
1 cup **white wine**
2 tablespoons **butter**
1/8 cup **brandy** (optional)
1 loaf **French bread,** cubed

1. In a bowl, combine all ingredients except bread and brandy. Place in a well-buttered 2-quart container. Cook 2 minutes, covered; rest 1 minute. Repeat until fondue has cooked 8 minutes.

2. Stir in brandy just before serving.

3. Serve by spearing cubed bread with fondue forks and dipping into hot fondue.

Makes 6-8 servings.

Kugel

8 ounces narrow **egg noodles**
1 cup **farmer cheese** or fine curd **cottage cheese**
4 **eggs,** beaten
1-1/2 cups unsweetened **applesauce**
2 tablespoons **lemon juice**
1/2 teaspoon dried **lemon peel**
1 tablespoon **butter,** melted
1 cup **sour cream**

1. Cook noodles. See guide (page 118). Drain and rinse.

2. In a bowl, combine all ingredients except noodles and sour cream.

3. Fold in noodles, Add sour cream and blend. In a greased 2-quart container, cook 10-12 minutes, covered. Let stand 10 minutes, covered.

Variations

A. Add 1/2 cup golden **raisins.**
B. Add 1/2 cup **dried apricots,** diced.
C. Substitute crushed **pineapple** for applesauce.

Makes 4-6 servings.

Cheese Manicotti or Canelloni

1 (8- to 10-ounce) box **manicotti or canelloni shells**
4 tablespoons dried **parsley flakes**
1/2 teaspoon **basil**
1/2 teaspoon **garlic powder**
3/4 cup canned **grated Parmesan cheese**
2 cups **ricotta cheese**
1 (8-ounce) package **cream cheese**
2 eggs, beaten
1 (1 1/8-ounce) envelope **chicken gravy mix**
Salt and **pepper** to taste
1 recipe **quick mornay sauce** (See page 45.)

1. Partially cook manicotti or canelloni shells. See guide (page 118). Drain and rinse.

2. In a bowl, combine remaining ingredients except mornay sauce.

3. Fill manicotti shells and place in a shallow, rectangular container. Pour half of the mornay sauce over the shells. Cook 7 minutes, loosely covered with wax paper. Turn shells over. Cover with remaining sauce. Cook 7 minutes, loosely covered with wax paper.

Makes 6-8 servings.

Tiered Cheese-and-Spinach Pancake

Pancake mix for 8-10 pancakes
1 egg

Make 8-10 pancakes according to package directions except add 1 egg. Cook on the microwave oven grill platter or conventionally.

Filling

2 (10-ounce) boxes frozen **chopped spinach,** thawed, drained
1 (8-ounce) package **cream cheese,** softened
1-1/2 cups **cheddar cheese,** grated

1. In a 1-quart container, place spinach. Cook 6-7 minutes, covered.

2. In a bowl, combine spinach, cream cheese, and cheddar cheese (save 1/2 cup cheddar cheese).

3. Layer the pancakes and cheese. Top with grated cheddar cheese. (Make 4-5 layers.)

4. Place on paper towel. Cook 4 minutes, uncovered. Rotate 1/4 turn every 60 seconds. Serve hot, cut in wedges.

Makes 6-8 servings.

Cream Cheese Filling for Pancakes

Dry **pancake mix** for 12 pancakes
2 **eggs**, beaten

1. Mix 12 pancakes according to package directions except use 2 eggs.

2. Cook pancakes in the microwave oven on grill platter or conventionally.

Topping

1 (8-ounce) package **cream cheese**, softened
1/2 cup **sugar**
1 teaspoon dried grated **lemon peel**
4 tablespoons **butter**, softened
2 **egg yolks**
1/4 cup **raisins**, chopped
1/4 cup **nuts**, chopped

1. On a paper plate, soften cream cheese. Cook 1 minute, uncovered.

2. In a bowl, combine all the ingredients. Cook 1 minute, uncovered. Stir after first 30 seconds.

3. Spread filling on pancakes. Place on a paper towel. Cook 30 seconds, uncovered. Serve hot.

Makes 12 servings.

NOTE: Make many small pancakes and serve as a brunch appetizer.

Cheese Rarebit

1 pound **tillamook cheese,** cubed
2 **eggs,** beaten
3/4 teaspoon **prepared mustard**
1/8 teaspoon **salt**
1 tablespoon **Worcestershire sauce**
3 drops **Tabasco sauce**
1/2 cup **beer** or more if needed
6 slices **toast** or 6 toasted **English muffins**

1. In a 2 1/2-quart container, cook cheese 4-6 minutes, uncovered.

2. Stir eggs into cheese and add remaining ingredients except toast. Cook 2 minutes or until bubbly hot.

3. Serve over toast or toasted English muffins.

Makes 6 servings.

Gruyère Strudel

1/2 pound **prepared strudel sheets**
1 cup **butter**

With a pastry brush, coat each strudel sheet with butter. Place one on top of the other on a floured board to make a rectangle. Cover with a damp cloth to keep moist.

Filling

2-1/4 cups **Gruyère cheese,** grated
2 **eggs,** beaten
1/2 teaspoon **nutmeg**
1/2 teaspoon **cinnamon**
2 tablespoons **butter,** melted
3/4 cup **whipping cream**

1. Combine all ingredients except 1/4 cup whipping cream. Spoon evenly over the strudel sheets.

2. Roll strudel up, jelly-roll fashion. With a pastry brush, coat strudel seam with water to fasten. Place seam side down in a buttered 7 x 12-inch container.

3. Cook 10-12 minutes, uncovered. Baste every 2 minutes with 1/4 cup whipping cream. Turn container 4 times during cooking period. Let stand 20 minutes or longer before cutting.

Makes 8 servings.

Eggs: Points to Remember

1. Do not boil eggs in the microwave oven; excess pressure will cause them to explode.
2. Soufflés or egg white-based recipes will not cook in the microwave oven; they need dry heat to expand.
3. Egg yolks cook faster than egg whites because of the high fat content. Cover eggs when cooking; take out eggs before the white has set because the steam will cook the white.
4. Overcooked eggs are tough and rubbery.
5. Mince overcooked fried egg and use as hard-cooked egg in dishes such as salads.
6. Salt sprinkled on eggs before cooking will help keep yolks from breaking.

Egg Guide

Fried Eggs

1/3 teaspoon butter
1 egg
Salt and pepper

1. Cook butter 5 seconds on a paper plate.

2. Add egg; salt and pepper to taste. Cover loosely with plastic wrap or another paper plate. Rotate 1/2 turn every 30 seconds.

3. Cover and let stand 1 minute.

1 egg cooks about 30 seconds.
2 eggs cook about 1 minute.
3 eggs cook about 1 minute 25-35 seconds.
4 eggs cook about 2 minutes.

Poached Eggs

1/4 cup water	Salt and pepper
1 egg	

1. In a custard cup, cook water 30 seconds.

2. Add egg; salt and pepper to taste. Cover tightly with plastic wrap. Cook 24-26 seconds. Let stand 1 minute, covered.

NOTE: Two eggs cook about 1 minute; 3 eggs cook 1 minute 25-30 seconds.

Scrambled Eggs

Use a soup bowl for 1-3 eggs and a 1-quart container for 4-6 eggs. Stir once.

NUMBER OF EGGS	BUTTER	HALF AND HALF	COOK	STIR	COOK
1	1 teaspoon	1 tablespoon	25-30 sec.	Yes	12-17 sec.
2	1-1/2 teaspoons	2 tablespoons	35-45 sec.	Yes	25-30 sec.
3	1 tablespoon	3 tablespoons	1 min. 5-10 sec.	Yes	35-45 sec.
4	1-1/2 tablespoons	4 tablespoons	1 min. 35-45 sec.	Yes	45-50 sec.
5	2 tablespoons	5 tablespoons	2 min.	Yes	1 min. 12-17 sec.
6	2-1/2 tablespoons	6 tablespoons	2 min. 20-25 sec.	Yes	1 min. 17-27 sec.

Eggs need different amounts of cooking time according to size, age, and temperature.

Accompaniment for Scrambled Eggs

The following recipes are for 6-8 eggs. All recipes may be mixed with the eggs at time of cooking.

Anchovies

1 (2-ounce) can **anchovies**

Mince anchovies.

Avocado

1/2 **lemon**

1 **avocado**, peeled, diced

Sprinkle lemon juice over avocado.

Bean Sprouts

1-1/2 cups fresh **bean sprouts**

1 tablespoon instant **minced onion**

1 tablespoon **soy sauce**

Combine all ingredients.

Cheese

1/4 to 1/2 cup **cheese** (grated if medium or hard)

1/4 cup frozen **chopped chives** or **green onion**

Combine all ingredients.

Chicken Liver

1/4 to 1/2 pound **chicken livers**, chopped

4 teaspoons **butter**, melted

3/4 tablespoon **tarragon**

In a 1/2-quart container, cook chicken livers in butter 2 minutes, uncovered. Stir every 30 seconds. Add tarragon; stir.

Corn and Crab Meat

1 (17-ounce) can **whole kernel corn**, drained
1 (6 1/2-ounce) can **crab meat**, flaked
1 teaspoon **curry powder**
2 tablespoons dried **parsley flakes**

Combine all ingredients.

Crab Meat

1 (7-ounce) can **crab meat**
1-1/2 tablespoons **sherry**

Combine all ingredients. Cook 1 minute, covered.

Denver

1 **tomato**, cut in pieces
1 (2-ounce) jar **pimentos**, chopped
1 cup **ham**, cooked, diced, or 1 cup **bacon**, cooked, crumbled

Combine all ingredients and add to eggs before cooking.

Mushroom Number One

1/2 pound fresh **mushrooms**, cleaned
4 tablespoons **butter**

1. Cut stems off mushrooms.

2. Fill caps with uncooked, scrambled egg mixture. Cook egg-filled mushroom caps in butter 2 minutes, loosely covered with wax paper.

Mushroom Number Two

1/4 to 1/2 pound fresh **mushrooms**, sliced
4 tablespoons **butter**

In a 1/2-quart container, cook mushrooms in butter 5 minutes, covered. Stir every 60 seconds. Add to eggs before cooking.

Sweetbreads

1/2 to 3/4 pound **sweetbreads,** diced
4 tablespoons **butter**

Sauté sweetbreads in butter. Cook 6 minutes; stir every 2 minutes.

Bacon-Wrapped Eggs in Cheese Sauce

8 eggs, hard cooked, peeled, cut lengthwise
1/2 cup **cheddar cheese,** grated
2 tablespoons frozen **chopped chives**
1 teaspoon **mustard**
1/2 teaspoon **celery salt**
Salt and **pepper** to taste
8 strips **bacon,** thin sliced
3/4 cup **beer**
1 (10 1/2-ounce) can **cheddar cheese soup**

1. In a bowl, combine egg yolks, cheese, chives, mustard, celery salt, and salt and pepper. Mince fine and put mixture back into the egg whites.

2. Press the 2 egg halves together. Wrap each egg with 1 bacon slice. Secure with toothpick.

3. On a paper towel, cook bacon-wrapped eggs, uncovered, until bacon is crisp. Turn often.

4. In a 1-quart container, combine beer and cheese soup. Cook 5 minutes, covered. Stir once. Pour over eggs in serving dish.

Makes 4 servings.

Curried Eggs

1 (10 1/2-ounce) can **white sauce**
3/4 teaspoon **curry powder** or to taste
1 teaspoon instant **minced onion**
Salt and **pepper** to taste
1 tablespoon **butter,** melted
12 **eggs,** hard cooked, peeled, cut lengthwise
6 **English muffins,** toasted

1. In a 1 1/2-quart container, combine all the ingredients except eggs and English muffins. Cook 3 minutes, covered. Add eggs; cook 2 minutes, covered.

2. Serve hot over toasted English muffins.

Makes 6 servings.

Basic Quiche

1 stick **pie dough mix**

Mix pie dough according to package directions. See Prepare Pastry (page 231). Use 9-inch pie plate or glass quiche plate.

Filling

1/4 cup **Gruyère or Swiss cheese,** grated
1/2 cup **onions,** chopped
1-1/2 cups **half and half**
1/8 teaspoon **nutmeg**
1/4 teaspoon **salt**
1/8 teaspoon **cayenne**
1/8 teaspoon **pepper**
2-3 **eggs,** beaten

1. Place cheese and onions in partially cooked pie shell.

2. In a 1-quart container, combine half and half and seasonings. Cook 2 minutes, uncovered. Stir every 30 seconds.

3. Slowly add beaten eggs; stir continuously. Pour over cheese and onions. Cook 7-8 minutes, uncovered. Rotate pie plate 1/4 turn every 2 minutes. Brown in microwave oven with browning element or conventionally. Let stand 10 minutes, uncovered.

Variations

A. Add to filling 5 slices cooked and crumbled **bacon.**
B. Add to filling 1 cup chopped **black olives.**
C. Replace onions with **chives.**
D. Add to filling 1 can **deviled ham.**
E. Use **leeks and garlic-flavored sausage** instead of onions.
F. Use (1) **milk** instead of cream; (2) 2 cups crumbled **feta cheese;** (3) 1/2 cup **onions.**

G. Add to filling 1 cup fresh or canned **mushrooms.**
H. Add to filling **shrimp, salmon, tuna,** or **crab meat.**
I. Add to filling **vegetables (peas, spinach, endive, corn,** or **more onions).**

Makes 6 servings.

Smoked Salmon and Eggs

3-4 **English muffins,** halved, toasted
6-8 slices **smoked salmon**
6-8 **eggs,** poached
1 recipe **cheese sauce** (See page 43.)

1. Place a slice of salmon on top of each muffin half.
2. Cook eggs. See guide (page 68). Place poached eggs over salmon.
3. Cook with hot cheese sauce.

Makes 6-8 servings.

NOTE: A slice of cooked Canadian bacon or bacon may replace the smoked salmon.

Seafood Eggs in Sour Cream

12 **eggs,** hard cooked, peeled, cut lengthwise
1 (6 1/2-ounce) can **crab meat** or 1 (6-ounce) box frozen **crab meat,** thawed, flaked
1/2 teaspoon **salt**
1/8 teaspoon **pepper**
1/2 tablespoon **dry mustard**
1/2 tablespoon **horseradish**
1/3 cup **sour cream**

1. Remove yolks and set aside.
2. In a bowl, combine crab, salt, pepper, mustard, and horseradish.
3. Stuff egg whites with the mixture. Place in a shallow container.
4. Crumble the yolks. Add to the sour cream. Pour over eggs. Cook 4-5 minutes, covered.

Makes 4-6 servings.

Fish: Points to Remember

1. Cook fish immediately before serving as they do not reheat well.
2. Cook fish covered; uncover last few minutes if stuffed or basted.
3. Fish cook fast and do not brown. Cook them until flaky; let stand one to two minutes, covered.
4. When browning is desired, either fry conventionally to brown or brown in the microwave oven with browning element last 60 seconds of cooking time.
5. Very small pieces of frozen fish can be thawed and cooked at the same time.

Fish Guide

Fresh Fish (1 lb.)

DIRECTIONS	TIME
Fish should be room temperature. In rectangular flat container, place 3 tablespoons melted butter. Add fish. Turn once.	4-5 min. or until flaky, covered. Stand 1-2 min., covered.

Fish Convenience Foods Guide

Boxed

NAME	AMOUNT	DIRECTIONS	TIME
Fish Seasoning Coating	2 oz.	Place seasonings in plastic sack with cut-up, washed fish filets (1 lb.); shake to coat. Place smaller pieces in the center.	
		Cook in 1-qt. container, uncovered. Turn once.	5 min. per lb.

Frozen

NAME	AMOUNT	DIRECTIONS	TIME
Breaded Fish Sticks or Kabobs	8 oz.	Arrange in a spoke pattern on paper towel.	1 min., uncovered. Stand 30 sec. Cook 2 min.
Breaded Whole Fish	7 oz.	Place on paper towel.	1 min. 30 sec., uncovered. Stand 30 sec. Cook 2 min., uncovered.
Tuna Pie	8 oz.	Remove from foil. Place in bowl about the size of the pie.	5-7 min., uncovered.
Whole Fish with or without Butter	11 oz.	Leave in styrofoam tray; slit plastic cover. Remove fish packaged in foil tray. Place in 1-qt. container, covered.	5-6 min., covered. With sauce 8-10 min., covered.

Fish Sticks Italiano

1 (1-pound) package frozen **precooked fish or clam sticks,** thawed
1 (15-ounce) jar **spaghetti sauce**
1 cup **pizza cheese,** shredded
4 tablespoons canned **grated Parmesan cheese**

1. In a 2-quart container, place fish or clam sticks.

2. Pour spaghetti sauce over the fish. Cook 5-6 minutes, covered.

3. Sprinkle cheeses over the top. Cook 1 minute, uncovered, or until melted.

Makes 4-6 servings.

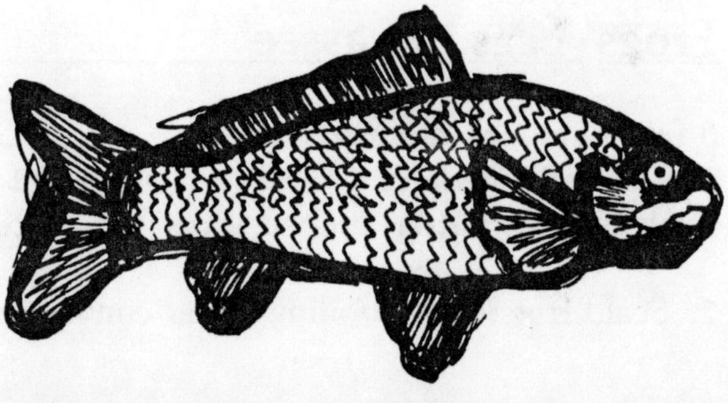

Stuffed Fish

1 (3- to 5-pound) fish, dressed and split
Salt and **pepper** to taste
4 tablespoons **butter**, melted
2 **lemons**, one halved and one eight-wedged

1. Salt and pepper inside of fish.
2. Squeeze juice from 1 lemon into melted butter.
3. Prepare stuffing.
4. Stuff fish; close opening with toothpicks. Place in a shallow container. Baste with lemon butter.
5. Cook 4-5 minutes per pound.
6. Serve with lemon wedges.

Stuffing

1 egg, beaten
1/8 teaspoon **thyme**
1/8 teaspoon **dill seed**
4 tablespoons dried **parsley flakes**
Dash **salt and pepper**
1/2 cup **butter**, melted
6 tablespoons **onion**, chopped
2 cups fine **bread crumbs**

1. In a bowl, combine egg and seasonings.
2. In a 1/2-quart container, sauté onion in butter; cook 1 minute, uncovered. Stir every 20 seconds. Add to egg mixture.
3. Mix in bread crumbs.

Makes 5-8 servings.

Frogs' Legs Fricassee

6 frog **hind legs**, skinned
1 quart boiling **water**
4 tablespoons **butter**, melted
1 cup **onions**, chopped
1 (10 1/2-ounce) can **white sauce**

1. Scald frog legs in boiling water conventionally.

2. Pour butter over frog legs in a 1-quart shallow container. Add onions. Pour white sauce over all.

3. Cook 6-7 minutes, covered. Rearrange once.

Makes 4-6 servings.

Fish Pie

1-1/2 pounds **fish**, flaked
4 tablespoons **sweet pickle**, chopped
1 teaspoon **salt**
1/8 teaspoon **pepper**
1-1/2 tablespoons **wine vinegar**
1 tablespoon instant **minced onion**
1 **tomato**, chopped
1 tablespoon dried **parsley flakes**
6 **filo or strudel sheets**
1/2 cup **butter**, melted

1. Cook fish. See guide (page 74).

2. In a bowl, combine all ingredients except filo or strudel sheets and butter.

3. With a pastry brush, coat each filo sheet with butter.

4. Place filo sheets in a square 2-quart container. Spread filling over the bottom.

5. Lap top of sheets over one another and coat with melted butter. Cook 9-12 minutes.

Makes 6-8 servings.

Haddock

1 (3 1/2- to 4-pound) **haddock**, head and tail trimmed, deboned
2 tablespoons **lemon juice**
Salt and **pepper** to taste

1. Pour lemon juice over the fish and sprinkle with salt and pepper. Cook in a bake-in-bag 3 minutes per pound.

2. Prepare stuffing.

3. Make a slit in the bag (watch for steam); add stuffing evenly over the fish. Form a mound in the center.

4. Cook 7-8 minutes, uncovered.

Stuffing

3/4 cup **unsalted crackers**
1 (2-ounce) can **mushrooms,** chopped
1/4 cup frozen **chopped chives**
1 tablespoon instant **minced onion**
1/2 tablespoon dried **parsley flakes**
1-1/2 teaspoons **seasoned salt**
1/8 teaspoon **pepper**
3/4 cup **butter,** melted
2 tablespoons **lemon juice**

In a bowl, combine all ingredients.

Makes 6-8 servings.

Hawaiian Halibut

1 (10 1/2-ounce) can **cream of shrimp soup**
3 teaspoons **chili sauce**
3/4 cup **macadamia nuts,** chopped
Salt and **pepper** to taste
1 pound **halibut**

1. In a 1/2-quart container, cook soup 4 minutes, covered.

2. Add the remaining ingredients except fish; stir; and pour over fish in a buttered, 2-quart flat container.

3. Cook 5-6 minutes or until fish flakes. (After first 3 minutes, check each minute.)

Makes 4-6 servings.

Scalloped Herring

1 (12-ounce) jar refrigerated **herring**
1 cup canned **white sauce**
1 tablespoon **lemon juice**
Salt and **pepper** to taste
Dash **Tabasco sauce**
1 tablespoon dried **parsley flakes**
8 tablespoons **butter,** melted
3/4 cup fine **bread crumbs**
1 **lemon,** quartered

1. Remove skin and bones. Flake.

2. In a bowl, mix fish with white sauce, lemon juice, salt, pepper, Tabasco sauce, and parsley flakes.

3. In another bowl, mix 4 tablespoons butter with bread crumbs. Press half the crumbs into 4 buttered scallop shells or 4 small salad plates, buttered.

4. Divide fish mixture between the scallop shells. Cover with remaining crumbs; pour butter over the top. Cook 3-4 minutes, loosely covered with wax paper.

5. Brown in the microwave oven with browning element or conventionally.

6. Garnish with lemon.

Makes 4 servings.

Spanish Paella

3 **Spanish sausages (charizos)**
2 (7-ounce) cans **lobster** or 2 (6-ounce) boxes frozen **lobster**
Salt and **pepper** to taste
2-1/2 cups **dry white wine**
1/2 pound **pork,** cubed
1/4 cup **olive oil**
2-1/4 cups hot **water**
1 (6-ounce) package **chicken-flavored rice**
1/2 teaspoon **saffron**
2 (8-ounce) cans **clams**
1 (8-ounce) can **oysters**
3 (5-ounce) cans **chicken**
6 tablespoons instant **minced onion**
6 teaspoons **sweet pepper flakes**
1 (15-ounce) can **tomatoes**
1 cup frozen **peas**
8 large **shrimp,** shelled, cleaned

1. Place 4 sheets of paper towels in a 2-quart container. Cook charizos 4 minutes, loosely covered with wax paper. Remove casing and towels.

2. Add lobster; cook 1 minute, covered.

3. Add salt and pepper and 2 tablespoons wine. Set aside.

4. In a 4-quart container, cook pork cubes in olive oil 4 minutes, loosely covered with wax paper. Stir every 2 minutes.

5. Add water, wine, rice, and saffron; cook 7 minutes, covered.

6. Add all ingredients except peas and shrimp; cook 7 minutes, covered.

7. Add peas and shrimp; cook 3 minutes, covered.

Makes 10-12 servings.

Salmon Loaf

1 (15 1/2-ounce) can **salmon**
1 (8 3/4-ounce) can **creamed corn**
3 tablespoons instant **minced onion**
2 **eggs,** beaten
3 tablespoons **butter,** melted
1 cup **milk**
Pepper to taste
24 **soda crackers,** crumbled

1. Combine salmon, corn, onion, eggs, butter, milk, and pepper.

2. Layer cracker crumbs and salmon mixture in a buttered glass loaf pan. Start and end with crumbs. Dot top with butter.

3. Cook 8-9 minutes, loosely covered with wax paper.

Makes 4-6 servings.

Singapore Fish

1 pound **cod or haddock**
Salt and **pepper** to taste

1. Cut fish in several pieces. Salt and pepper. Place in 2-quart container.

2. Pour sauce over fish and cook 5-7 minutes, covered.

Sauce

1-1/4 cups canned or fresh refrigerated **coconut milk**
1 teaspoon dried **red chili flakes** or more to taste
1/8 teaspoon dried **powdered coriander**
1/4 teaspoon dried **powdered cumin**
1 teaspoon **garlic powder**
1 cup **onions**, chopped
1/4 teaspoon **tumeric**
2 tablespoons **vegetable oil**

Puree the ingredients in a blender or use electric mixer.

Makes 4-6 servings.

Italian Trout

6 tablespoons **butter,** melted
4 **trout,** room temperature
1 (1 1/2-ounce) package **shake-n-bake** and plastic sack
3 **green onions** and **tops,** chopped
4 tablespoons dried **parsley flakes**
1 (4-ounce) can **mushrooms,** sliced, drained
1/2 teaspoon dried **Italian seasoning** or 1/8 teaspoon **oregano**
2 **lemons,** quartered, to garnish

1. Use a pastry brush to coat trout with butter.

2. Place trout in shake-n-bake sack. Add the seasoning, crumbs, onions, parsley, and mushrooms and shake gently.

3. In a 2-quart container, cook 4-5 minutes per pound, loosely covered with wax paper.

4. Garnish with lemon wedges.

Makes 4 servings.

Tuna-Corn Casserole

1/4 cup **butter**
1/2 (10-ounce) package frozen **carrots**, thawed
1/2 cup **celery**
2 tablespoons instant **minced onion**
1 (10 1/2-ounce) can **potato soup**
2 (6 1/2-ounce) cans **tuna**, drained, flaked
1 (17-ounce) can **cream-style corn**
1/8 teaspoon dried **rosemary**
1/4 cup frozen **chopped chives**
Few drops **Tabasco sauce**

1. In a 2 1/2-quart container, cook carrots, celery, and onion in butter 4 minutes, uncovered. Stir every 30 seconds.

2. Add the remaining ingredients. Cook 7-9 minutes, covered.

Makes 4-6 servings.

Leftovers

Think positive about leftovers. When you cook the microwave method, no one can tell your food sat in the refrigerator overnight. Save the food moisture by covering the food container tightly with plastic wrap. You can serve your food items exactly as you prepared them, or follow recipes in this book to create a new image for yesterday's dinner.

Leftovers: Points to Remember

1. Cover vegetables, casseroles, meats, poultry, fish, and shellfish with plastic wrap or place in a small covered container.

2. Rearrange or stir large food quantities during cooking time.

3. Large food items should have one or two standing periods during cooking time.

4. Cooking time increases as quantity increases.

Leftover Guide

Salads

1 salad	1-2 min.
1 serving	15-30 sec.

Casseroles, Rice, Noodles, Soups, and Vegetables

1 cup	1-2 min.
2 cups	2-3 min.
3 cups	3-4 min.
4 cups	4-5 min.
5 cups	6-7 min.

Meats and Poultry

1 slice or piece	30 sec. to 1 min.
2 slices or pieces	1 min. to 1 min. 30 sec.
3 slices or pieces	1 min. 30 sec. to 2 min.
4 slices or pieces	2 min. to 2 min. 30 sec.
6 slices or pieces	3 min. to 3 min. 30 sec.
8 slices or pieces	4 min.
12 slices or pieces	5-6 min.

Keep meat slices as thin and as even as possible. Cover with plastic wrap. When using cooked meat in a casserole, the cooking time usually depends on the cooking time of the other ingredients. There is little chance of overcooking the meat.

NOTE: Fish and shellfish by themselves do not reheat as well as meats and poultry. Pour 1/2 teaspoon water over each serving and cook as for meats and poultry. Cover with plastic wrap. See guides (pages 184, 199, and 233) for breads and desserts.

Eggs

1 egg	30 sec.
2 eggs	40-45 sec.
3 eggs	1 min. to 1 min. 10 sec.
4 eggs	1 min. 40 sec.

NOTE: These times are only approximate.

Beef-in-Spaghetti Sour Cream Sauce

1 (8-ounce) package **medium noodles**
3 tablespoons **butter**, melted
3-4 cups **roast beef**, cooked, cut in thin strips
3 tablespoons **butter**
4 tablespoons instant **minced onion**
1 (1 1/2-ounce) envelope **spaghetti sauce mix**
1 (15-ounce) can **tomato puree**
1 (4-ounce) can sliced **mushrooms**
1 cup **sour cream**
4 tablespoons dried **parsley flakes**

1. Cook noodles. See guide (page 118). Drain and rinse. Stir in butter.

2. In a 2-quart container, cook beef in butter 2 minutes, covered. Stir after first 60 seconds.

3. Add onion, spaghetti sauce mix, tomato puree, mushrooms, and parsley; stir. Cook 4 minutes, covered.

4. Stir in sour cream. Cook 1 minute 30 seconds, uncovered. Stir every 30 seconds.

Makes 6-8 servings.

Chicken, Turkey, or Ham Divan

2 (10-ounce) packages frozen **broccoli**
1 (10 1/2-ounce) can **cream of chicken soup**
2 or more cups **chicken, turkey,** or **ham**, cooked, diced
1 cup **sour cream**
1 cup **cheddar cheese**, shredded

1. Cook broccoli. See guide (page 163).

2. In a 2-quart container, cook cream of chicken soup 3 minutes, covered. Stir once.

3. Add poultry or ham. Cook 2-3 minutes, covered. Stir once.

4. Add sour cream, broccoli, and 1/2 cup cheese; stir. Cook 2 minutes, covered. Top with remaining cheese. Cook 1 minute, uncovered.

5. Let stand 3 minutes, covered.

Makes 6-8 servings.

NOTE: For each extra cup poultry or ham, add 2 minutes cooking time at step 3.

Turkey Chili

2 tablespoons **vegetable oil**
1 cup **onions**, diced
4 tablespoons dried **sweet pepper flakes**
1 (4-ounce) can **mushrooms**, drained
2 cups or more **turkey**, diced
1 (1 3/4-ounce) envelope **chili mix**
4 (15-ounce) cans **tomato sauce**
1 (15-ounce) can **whole tomatoes**

1. In a 4-quart container, cook onions, pepper flakes, and mushrooms in oil 2 minutes, uncovered. Stir every 30 seconds.

2. Add remaining ingredients; stir. Cook 10-12 minutes or until hot, covered. Stir every 3 minutes.

Makes 6-8 servings.

NOTE: For each extra cup turkey, add 2 minutes cooking time at step 2.

Filled Pancakes

dry **pancake mix** for 8 pancakes
2 **eggs**, beaten
soup or sauce

1. Make 8 thin pancakes according to package directions except add eggs. Cook pancakes on microwave oven grill platter or conventionally.

2. Place 4-5 tablespoons of the filling on each pancake. Roll up; place in a shallow container, seam side down.

3. Cover filled pancakes with a hot cheese sauce, hot mornay sauce, or 1 (10 1/2-ounce) can condensed chicken soup, condensed mushroom soup, or shrimp soup. Cook soup 4 minutes in a 1-quart glass measure.

4. Cook 3-4 minutes in a shallow container, covered loosely with wax paper.

Makes 8 servings.

Filling Variations

Fish Filling

2 (7-ounce) cans **tuna**, flaked, or 2 cups **fish**, cooked, flaked
1/4 cup **tomato puree**
3 tablespoons instant **minced onion**
2 tablespoons dried **parsley flakes**
1 tablespoon **chutney**, diced (optional)
4 tablespoons **celery**, diced
Salt and **pepper** to taste

1. In a bowl, combine all ingredients.
2. Cook 5 minutes, covered. Stir every 60 seconds.

Shellfish Filling

2 cups **shellfish**
1 cup **celery**, diced
1/2 cup **almonds**, slivered
1/2 cup **mayonnaise**
1/3 cup **sour cream**
1 tablespoon **lemon juice**
1/8 teaspoon **salt**

In a bowl, combine all ingredients.

Meat Filling

1 (3/4-ounce) envelope **red wine gravy mix** or **beef gravy mix**
2 cups **meat**, diced
2 tablespoons **onion**, minced
2 tablespoons dried **parsley flakes**
1 tablespoon **concentrated beef tea** or instant **beef bouillon**
Salt and **pepper** to taste

1. Prepare gravy mix according to package directions.
2. In a bowl, combine all ingredients.

Poultry Filling

1 (3/4-ounce) envelope **white wine gravy mix** or 1 (7/8-ounce) envelope **chicken gravy mix**
2 cups **poultry, diced**
1/8 teaspoon **sage**
Salt and **pepper** to taste
1 **egg,** hard cooked, minced (optional)

1. Prepare gravy mix according to package directions.
2. In a bowl, combine all ingredients; stir.

Greek Lamb Pie

1/2 (7 1/2-ounce) package **risseto mix**
16 **filo dough sheets**
1/4 cup **butter,** melted
1 cup instant **potato flakes**
2 cups **lamb,** cooked, cubed
3 **eggs,** hard cooked, quartered
1-1/2 cups **feta cheese,** crumbled
1/2 teaspoon dried **lemon peel**
1 teaspoon dried **mint flakes**
2 tablespoons dried **parsley flakes**
Salt and **pepper** to taste
1/8 teaspoon **oregano**
3 tablespoons **lemon juice**
2 tablespoons **olive oil**
1/2 cup **lamb broth** or 1/2 cup **bouillon**
1 **egg,** beaten

1. Cook risetto according to package directions.
2. Line a 7 x 5 x 2-inch container with 8 filo dough sheets. Place 1 sheet at a time. Use a pastry brush to spread butter on each sheet.
3. Prepare mashed potatoes according to package directions. See guide (page 167).
4. Layer risseto, lamb, potatoes, eggs, and cheese on top of the filo dough sheets. Sprinkle with seasonings.
5. In a cup, combine lemon juice, oil, broth, and beaten egg. Pour over the filling.

6. Top with remaining filo dough sheets.

7. Cook 5-6 minutes, loosely covered with wax paper. Rotate 1/4 turn every 2 minutes.

8. Brown in the microwave oven with browning element or conventionally.

Makes 6-8 servings.

Shepherd's Pie

3 tablespoons **butter**
3/4 cup **onions**, chopped
1 (3/4-ounce) envelope **brown gravy mix**
2 cups **lamb**, cooked, fat removed, cut in small pieces
1/8 teaspoon **thyme**
1 teaspoon **salad herbs**
2 tablespoons **catsup**
1 **carrot**, minced
1/2 cup **celery**, minced
Salt and **pepper** to taste
2 cups instant **potato flakes**

1. In a 1-quart container, cook onions in butter 3 minutes, uncovered. Stir every 30 seconds.

2. Prepare gravy according to package directions. Add to onions; stir. Cook 1 minute 30 seconds. Stir every 30 seconds.

3. In a deep 3-quart greased container, combine the remaining ingredients except potatoes. Pour gravy over meat mixture; stir. Cook 4-5 minutes, covered.

4. Prepare mashed potatoes according to package directions. See guide (page 167).

5. Cover meat mixture with potatoes. Cook 1-2 minutes, covered. Let stand 5 minutes, covered.

Makes 4-6 servings.

NOTE: Other leftover meat may be substituted for the lamb.

Chinese Pork

Up to 12 thin slices of **pork roast**, cooked
1 cup uncooked **rice**

1. Prepare sauce.

2. Use a pastry brush to coat each pork slice with sauce. Place on wax paper; cook 3 minutes 30 seconds to 4 minutes, uncovered. Turn over after first 2 minutes.

Sauce

1/3 cup **soy sauce**
1 cup **water**
1 cube **chicken bouillon**
1 teaspoon **garlic salt**
1/2 teaspoon **vinegar**

In a 1/2-quart container, combine ingredients. Cook 3 minutes, covered. Stir every 30 seconds. (The bouillon cube will dissolve as you stir.)

Makes 4 servings.

NOTE: Chinese Pork is good served over rice or canned or frozen Chinese vegetables.

Turkey Spaghetti

1 (4-ounce) package **spaghetti**
1 (10 1/2-ounce) can **cream of mushroom soup**
1-1/3 cup **milk**
1 (17-ounce) can **whole kernel corn**
1-1/2 to 2 cups **turkey**, cooked, diced
1 teaspoon **salt**
1/4 cup **bread crumbs**

1. Cook spaghetti. See guide (page 118). Drain and rinse.

2. In a greased 1-1/2 quart container, combine soup, milk, corn, turkey, and salt.

3. Mix spaghetti into the sauce. Sprinkle with bread crumbs.

4. Cook 8-10 minutes, covered. Let stand 5 minutes, covered.

Makes 4-6 servings.

NOTE: Chicken or tuna fish may be substituted for the turkey.

Meats: Points to Remember

Chops

1. Cook five to six chops 25-30 minutes.
2. Do not fry chops in the microwave oven. Cook chops in sauce or stuffed.

Cubed Meats

1. Pork, lamb, and veal are tender. When used in a casserole, they cook in the same amount of time as the other ingredients.
2. Beef cubes need to be tenderized before using in a casserole or skewered.

Ground Meats

1. Grinding tenderizes meats.
2. All ground meats take about the same amount of time to cook. Cook five minutes, loosely covered with wax paper, for one pound of meat. Meat will be crumbly as when fried.

Hams and Ham Slices

1. Canned ham is already cooked; only reheat, allowing six minutes per pound as a guide.

Pork Ribs

1. Cook 12-15 minutes, covered loosely with wax paper, for three to four pounds.
2. Siphon off fat.
3. Add sauce and cook eight to ten minutes, covered.

Roasts

1. Start at room temperature.
2. Because meat bones keep the microwaves from penetrating, cover bones with foil.
3. The tenderer the meat, the faster it cooks.

4. Cook even-shaped roasts if possible. If the thickness of a roast is inconsistent, the thinner portion must be covered with foil the first half of the cooking time to keep that portion from overcooking.
5. NEVER LET THE FOIL TOUCH THE OVEN CAVITY. It can ruin your microwave oven.
6. Pot roasts and the other less tender cuts need a 25-minute standing time after half the cooking time.
7. Test temperature with meat thermometer after the meat has completed its standing time. NEVER PUT MEAT THERMOMETER IN OVEN.
8. You can completely cook roasts in the microwave oven or cook roasts the microwave method for the first half of cooking time and finish cooking conventionally.

Steaks

1. Rib and sirloin cook quickly in the microwave oven. Use microwave browning grill plates or cook in a sauce.
2. Tenderize round and chuck before using.
3. Tomato, wine, and other acidic foods used in the recipes help to tenderize meat.

NOTE: FOLLOW YOUR MANUFACTURER'S INSTRUCTIONS FOR THE USE OF ALUMINUM FOIL.

Meat Guide

AMOUNT	TIME (AT ROOM TEMPERATURE)
8 oz.	1 min. 30 sec. to 2 min.
15 oz.	2 min. 30 sec. to 3 min.
24 oz.	4 min. to 4 min. 30 sec.
32 oz.	5 min. to 5 min. 30 sec.
40 oz.	7-8 min.

NOTE: When food item is frozen, add 4-7 minutes.

Bacon Guide

DIRECTIONS	TIME (DEPENDS ON THICKNESS OF BACON)
1 strip	1 min. 30 sec.
2 strips	1 min. 15 sec. to 1 min. 48 sec.
3 strips	2 min. 20 sec.
4 strips	3 min.

Place between two paper towels.

Roasting Guide

MEAT	DIRECTIONS	MINUTES PER POUND	STANDING TIME	TEMPERATURE
Beef	Rare	5-6	30-40 min.	130-140°
	Medium	6-7		150-160°
	Well-done	7-8		170°
	Turn once. Cover bones with foil.			
	If roast is long, cover ends with foil. Don't let foil touch the bottom of the cavity. Remove foil after half cooking time.			
Lamb Leg or Shoulder	Medium	7 to 7-1/2	30-40 min.	160-170°
	Well-done	8 to 8-1/2		175-180°
	If bone is in, wrap last 2 in. with foil. Don't let foil touch cavity. Remove foil after half cooking time. Turn twice.			
Pork				
Ham				
Canned 3-5 lb.	Remove gelatin. Turn once. Glaze last 5 min.	5-7	20-30 min.	130°

MEAT	DIRECTIONS	MINUTES PER POUND	STANDING TIME	TEMPERATURE
Canned 8-10 lb.	Remove gelatin. Turn once. Glaze last 5 min.	7-9	40-45 min.	130°
Fully Cooked	Cook fat side down. Rotate 4 times. Glaze last 5 min.	7-9	30-60 min.	130°
Ham Shoulder		9-10	30-45 min.	185°
Fresh Pork		8-9	15-20 min.	170°
Veal	Cover top with bacon. Cook half time. Turn. Cover with bacon. Finish cooking.	8-10	30 min.	165-170°

Frozen Meat Convenience Foods Guide

NAME	AMOUNT	DIRECTIONS	TIME
Barbecued Ribs	32 oz.	Cook in plastic container.	1 min.
		When soft, place in shallow container. Turn twice.	6 min. Cover with wax paper.
Beef Enchiladas	32 oz.	Remove from foil container. Place in 3-qt. container.	12-14 min., covered.
Beef, Macaroni, and Tomatoes	11 oz.	Remove from foil container. Place in 1-qt. container. Turn twice.	7-9 min., covered.
Cabbage Rolls, Stuffed	14 oz.	Remove from foil container. Place in 1-qt. container. Turn twice.	7-8 min., covered.
Creamed Chipped Beef	14 oz.	Cook in container. Stir once.	6-7 min. Cover with wax paper.
Green Chili Burritos	12 oz.	Place on paper towel.	5-7 min., uncovered.

Main Dishes-Meats

NAME	AMOUNT	DIRECTIONS	TIME
Green Pepper Steak with Rice	10-1/2 oz.	Remove from foil container. Place in 1-qt. container.	5-7 min. 30 sec., covered.
Meat Loaf	24 oz.	Remove from foil container. Place in glass loaf pan.	8 min. Stand 5 min. Cook 5 min Stand 5 min. Cover with wax paper.
Roast Beef Hash	11-1/2 oz.	Remove from foil container. Place in 1-qt. container.	6-8 min., covered.
Short Ribs of Beef	11 oz.	Remove from foil container. Place in 1 1/2-qt. container. Turn twice.	9-11 min., covered.
Sliced Beef and Giblet Gravy	32 oz.	Remove from foil container. Place in 3-qt. container.	12-14 min., covered.
Sloppy Joe	26 oz.	Remove from foil container. Place in 2-qt. container.	8-11 min., covered.
Stuffed Peppers	32 oz.	Remove from foil container. Place in 3-qt. container.	12-14 min., covered.
Sweet-and-Sour Pork	14 oz.	Remove from foil container. Place in 1-qt. container.	7-9 min., covered.
Mushroom Sauce and Sirloin Tips	8 oz.	Remove from foil container. Place in 1/2-qt. container.	5-7 min., covered.
Veal Parmigiana	32 oz.	Remove from foil container. Place in 3-qt. container.	12-14 min., covered.

NOTE: Subtract 3-4 minutes when food item is at room temperature.

Heating Precooked Frozen Meat Casseroles

When heating precooked frozen meats and meat casseroles not listed on the Frozen Meat Convenience Foods Guide, follow the Meat Guide (see page 91). Cover, stir, or rearrange at least once during heating period to speed and evenly distribute the cooking. Allow large food items, such as meat loaf, to stand once during heating time.

Beef Biscuit Casserole

1-1/2 pounds **ground beef**
1 cup **celery,** minced
3/4 cup **onions,** chopped
2 tablespoons dried **sweet green peppers**
1 teaspoon **garlic powder**
1 (6-ounce) can **tomato paste**
1 (12-ounce) package frozen **hash brown potatoes,** thawed
3/4 cup **water**
Salt and **pepper** to taste
1 tablespoon **paprika**
1 (16-ounce) can **pork and beans,** undrained
1 (15-ounce) can **green beans**
2 (8-ounce) packages refrigerated **biscuits**
1/3 cup **pimento-stuffed olives**
1/3 cup **almonds,** blanched, slivered

1. In a shallow 3-quart container, combine meat, celery, onions, peppers, and garlic powder. Cook 5 minutes, covered. Stir every 30 seconds.

2. Add tomato paste, potatoes, water, salt, pepper, paprika, pork and beans, and green beans; stir. Reserve 1 cup. Cook 6 minutes, covered. Stir twice.

3. On a lightly floured breadboard, combine 2 packages refrigerated biscuits. Knead together and roll out in a 12 x 8-inch rectangle.

4. Combine pimento-stuffed olives and almonds with the 1 cup reserved meat mixture. Spread over the top of the dough. Roll up, lengthwise, jelly-roll fashion; pinch together. Cut in 1-inch pieces; place on top of meat mixture.

5. Cook 12-14 minutes, uncovered.

Makes 8-10 servings.

Fast Dried Beef Casserole

1 (5-ounce) jar **dried beef**
3/4 cup **celery,** diced
1 (10-ounce) package frozen **peas**
1 (10 1/2-ounce) can **cream of mushroom soup**
1 (10 1/2-ounce) can **cream of chicken soup**
2 tablespoons instant **minced onion**
1/4 teaspoon **garlic powder**
1 (5-ounce) can **chow mein noodles**

1. Tear beef into strips.

2. In a bowl, combine all ingredients, except chow mein noodles.

3. In a shallow 2-quart container, add beef and soup mixture to 1/2 of noodles.

4. Cook 8 minutes, covered. Stir once. Add remaining noodles; cook 3 minutes, uncovered.

Makes 4-6 servings.

Beef Enchiladas

1-1/4 pounds **ground beef**
1 cup **onions,** chopped
1 dozen **corn tortillas**
1/2 cup **vegetable oil**
1 pound **tillamook or cheddar cheese,** grated

1. Prepare sauce.

2. In a 2-quart container, cook ground beef and onions 5 minutes. Stir every 2 minutes. Siphon off fat.

3. Conventionally fry corn tortillas in oil on both sides. (They should be limp.)

4. Dip tortillas into sauce. Place on a large flat container. Sprinkle each tortilla with cheddar cheese. Spoon meat mixture over top.

5. Fold and place, seam side down, in a lightly greased, shallow 2 1/2-quart container.

6. Sprinkle with remaining cheddar cheese. Pour remaining sauce over the top. Cook 3 minutes 30 seconds, covered. Rotate container 1/2 turn after the first 2 minutes.

Sauce

4 tablespoons **shortening**
1/2 cup **flour**
1/2 teaspoon **paprika**
1/8 teaspoon **celery salt**
1/2 teaspoon **garlic**
1/2 teaspoon **salt**
1/2 teaspoon **chili powder**
1/8 teaspoon **oregano**
1 (6-ounce) can **tomato paste**
3 cups **water**
2 (10-ounce) cans **chili sauce**

1. In a deep 2-quart container, cook shortening 30 seconds, uncovered.

2. Stir flour into oil to make a paste.

3. Add the remaining ingredients; stir until smooth. Cook 7-9 minutes, covered. Stir twice.

Makes 4-6 servings.

NOTE: One envelope (1-5/8 ounces) enchilada sauce mix and 3 cups water may be substituted for sauce recipe.

Meat Manicotti or Canelloni

1 (8- to 10-ounce) box **manicotti or canelloni shells**
1-1/2 pounds **beef, ground**
4 tablespoons dried **parsley flakes**
1/2 teaspoon **basil**
1/2 teaspoon **garlic powder**
1/2 cup canned **grated Parmesan cheese**
1/2 cup **Italian cooking sauce**
2 **eggs, beaten**
1 (7/8-ounce) envelope **chicken gravy mix**
Salt and **pepper** to taste
1 recipe **quick mornay sauce** (See page 45.)

1. Partially cook manicotti or canelloni shells. See guide (page 118). Drain and rinse.

2. In a bowl, combine remaining ingredients except mornay sauce.

3. Fill manicotti shells. Place them in a shallow, rectangular container. Pour half of the mornay sauce over the shells. Cook 7 minutes, loosely covered with wax paper. Turn shells over. Cover with remaining sauce. Cook 7 minutes, loosely covered with wax paper.

Makes 6-8 servings.

Mexican Casa Casserole

1 (16-ounce) package **noodles**
1-1/4 pounds **ground beef**
1/4 pound **ground pork** or cubed leftover pieces **pork**
2 cups frozen **corn**
1 (15-ounce) can **hominy,** drained
2 cups **cheddar cheese,** grated
1 (15-ounce) can **chili con carne**
1/2 cup canned **tamale sauce**
1 (10 1/2-ounce) can **tomato soup**
2 tablespoons **vegetable oil**

1. Cook noodles. See guide (page 118). Drain and rinse.

2. In a 3-quart container, cook ground beef and ground pork. Cook 6 minutes, covered. Stir every 60 seconds. Siphon off grease.

3. Add the remaining ingredients except 1/4 cup cheddar cheese.

4. Sprinkle cheddar cheese over the top. Cook 10-12 minutes, covered. Stir every 3 minutes.

Makes 6-8 servings.

Fruited Pot Roast

1 3- to 4-pound **pot roast**
2-1/2 cups **Burgundy wine**
1 **carrot,** chopped
1/2 cup **onions,** chopped
1/2 teaspoon **garlic powder**
Salt and **pepper** to taste
1 (12-ounce) package **mixed dried fruit**

1. In a 4-quart container, cook pot roast 10 minutes, uncovered.

2. Add the remaining ingredients. (Dried fruit should float in the wine.)

3. Cook 25 minutes, loosely covered with wax paper. Turn meat over once during cooking period. Let stand 20 minutes, covered.

4. Serve with fruit on top of meat. Pour pan juices over meat.

Makes 4-6 servings.

Pepper Steak

1 pound **round steak,** 1/2 inch thick, cut in long diagonal strips
3 tablespoons **vegetable oil**
2 tablespoons instant **minced onion**
3 **green peppers,** chopped
1-1/4 cup **consommé**
1/4 teaspoon powdered **ginger**
1 tablespoon **soy sauce**

1. Conventionally brown steak in oil.

2. In a 3-quart container, cook all ingredients 15-17 minutes, covered. Stir every 5 minutes.

Makes 2 servings.

Steak and Bacon Bits

5 or more slices **bacon,** cut in 3 equal parts
2 tablespoons instant **minced onion**
1 pound **round steak** 1/2 inch thick, cut in 2-inch squares
1 cup **flour**
2-3 tablespoons **vegetable oil** or **bacon grease**
1 (7/8-ounce) envelope **beef gravy mix** or 1 **bouillon cube** and 1 cup **water**
1 (10-ounce) package frozen **sliced carrots,** thawed

1. Place a small piece of bacon and a few minced onions on top of a beef square. Roll up and fasten with a toothpick.

2. Dredge meat in flour.

3. In a 2-quart container, cook the oil 20 seconds. Add the meat; cook 3 minutes, uncovered. Turn as needed.

4. In a bowl, prepare the beef gravy according to package directions. Pour over the meat. Add the carrots.

5. Cook 10-12 minutes, covered. Remove toothpicks before serving.

Makes 2-4 servings.

Saucy Chuck Steak

Sauce

1 package **onion soup mix**
2-1/2 tablespoons **brown sugar**
1/4 teaspoon **lemon pepper**
1 tablespoon **prepared mustard**
3/4 cup **catsup**
1/4 cup **white wine**
1/8 teaspoon **fennel**
1 cup **water**

1. In a 2-quart container, combine all ingredients.

2. Cook 5 minutes, covered. Stir 2 times during cooking period.

1 (4-pound) **chuck steak**
1/2 inch thick, tenderized,
cut in diagonal strips
2 tablespoons **vegetable oil**

1. Conventionally brown meat in oil.

2. Add meat to sauce. Cook 10 minutes, covered. Let stand 20 minutes, covered. Cook 5 minutes, covered. Rearrange every 2 minutes during cooking periods.

Makes 4-6 servings.

Steak Tartar Bake

2 pounds **sirloin** or **tenderloin,** free of fat, ground twice
1 cup **onions,** chopped
2 tablespoons **garlic powder**
4 tablespoons frozen **chopped chives**
1 to 2 teaspoons **salt**
Lemon-pepper
3/4 cup dried **parsley flakes**
1/2 cup **walnuts,** toasted, chopped
8 **anchovy filets**
2 **lemons,** cut in wedges

1. In a bowl, combine steak, onions, garlic powder, chives, salt, pepper, and parsley.

2. Divide into 4 or 8 patties or 35-45 meatballs.

3. Place walnuts in a flat, ungreased container. Cook 2 minutes, uncovered. Stir every 30 seconds.

4. Roll the patties in the hot walnuts to form a coating.

5. Cook covered loosely with wax paper. See guide (page 142). Place an anchovy filet on each patty 1 minute before done.

6. Garnish with lemon wedges.

Makes 6-8 servings.

Stew Casserole

3-1/4 pounds **beef,** cut in 1 1/2-inch cubes
2-1/2 tablespoons **vegetable oil**
1 (7/8-ounce) envelope **brown gravy mix**
1 (1 1/2-ounce) envelope **stew mix**
1 (2-ounce) can **mushrooms,** chopped
2 tablespoons **paprika**
1 **bay leaf**
4 drops **Tabasco sauce**
Salt and **pepper** to taste
1 (10-ounce) package frozen **carrots,** thawed
1 (10-ounce) package frozen **whole okra,** thawed
1/2 cup **onions,** chopped
1 (10-ounce) package frozen **hash brown potatoes,** thawed

1. In a 3-quart container, sauté beef in oil. Cook 8 minutes, uncovered. Stir every 60 seconds.

2. Prepare gravy mix according to package directions. Add to meat with remaining ingredients; stir.

3. Cook 12 minutes, covered. Stir every 3 minutes.

Makes 6-8 servings.

Tamale Pie

2 **tamales,** cut in pieces
2 (15-ounce) cans **chili,** one with beans, one without
1 (16-ounce) can **cream-style corn**
3 tablespoons instant **minced onion**
1-1/2 cups **cheddar cheese,** shredded
1 (6-ounce) can **black olives** (optional)

1. In a 2 1/2-quart container, layer all the ingredients except olives. End with a layer of cheese.

2. Cook 12 minutes, covered. Uncover; cook 3 minutes.

3. Garnish with black olives.

Makes 4-6 servings.

Stuffed Breast of Lamb

2-pound boned **breast of lamb**
Salt and **pepper** to taste
1/2 teaspoon **garlic salt**
3 tablespoons **flour**
2 tablespoons **butter,** melted
1 cup **apples,** peeled, cored, diced
1/4 pound **ground sausage**
4 tablespoons dried **parsley flakes**
1/8 teaspoon **rosemary**
2 tablespoons dried **mint leaves**

1. Sprinkle salt, pepper, and garlic salt on lamb. Dredge in flour.

2. In a bowl, combine remaining ingredients and spread over the inside of lamb.

3. Roll up and tie with string. Place in a plastic bake-in-bag. Slit bag. Cook 20 minutes; turn 4 times. Let stand 30 minutes, covered.

Makes 2-4 servings.

Curried Lamb Kabobs

18 pieces **lamb,** cubed
6 slices **bacon**
18 **dates,** pitted
18 small **onions** or 3 large **onions,** cut in pieces
1 **green pepper,** cut in 1-inch squares
4 bamboo **skewers**

1. Prepare sauce.

2. Pour sauce over the cubed lamb. Let stand 4 hours or more. Turn to coat all sides.

3. Cut the bacon slices in 3 equal parts. Wrap the dates in the bacon.

4. Skewer the meat, onions, green papper, and bacon-wrapped dates.

5. On wax paper, place meat in spoke pattern. Cook 7-10 minutes, uncovered. Baste with sauce every 2 minutes and turn. Let stand 12 minutes, covered.

Sauce

6 tablespoons **butter**
1 tablespoon **cornstarch**
1 cup hot **water**
1/2 teaspoon **onion salt**
1 teaspoon **curry powder**
1 teaspoon **sugar**
1/8 teaspoon **saffron**
4 tablespoons **white vinegar**

1. In a 1-quart container, cook butter 30 seconds.

2. Stir in cornstarch to make a paste.

3. Add water slowly; stir constantly.

4. Add the remaining ingredients; stir.

5. Cook 3 minutes, covered. Stir every 30 seconds. Cool.

Makes 4 servings.

Lamb Curry

2 pounds **lamb,** cubed
2 tablespoons **olive oil**
1 cup **onions,** chopped
1 teaspoon **garlic powder**
1 **apple,** peeled, cored, sliced
1-1/2 teaspoons **curry powder**
1/8 teaspoon **saffron**
4 drops **Tabasco sauce**
1 teaspoon **lemon juice**
1 (7/8-ounce) envelope **chicken gravy mix**
1 cup hot **water**
1 **tomato,** minced
2 cups cooked **rice**

1. In a 2-quart container, cook meat in oil 5 minutes, uncovered. Stir every 60 seconds.

2. Add the onions, garlic powder, and apple. Cook 4 minutes, covered. Stir every 60 seconds. Add seasonings.

3. In a bowl, dissolve gravy mix in water; stir. Pour over meat. Add tomato; stir.

4. Cook 8-10 minutes, covered. Let stand 5 minutes, covered.

5. Pour Lamb Curry over rice.

Makes 4-8 servings.

Lamb Riblets Number One

2 pounds **riblets**
1/2 cup **water**
4 tablespoons instant **minced onion**
2 (2-ounce) envelopes **sweet-and-sour sauce mix**

1. In a 2 1/2-quart container, place riblets in water; sprinkle minced onion over the top. Cook 18-20 minutes, covered. Rearrange meat twice during cooking period.

2. Prepare sauce according to package directions; pour over riblets.

3. Cook 4-5 minutes, uncovered. Rearrange and baste every minute. Rearrange and let stand 5 minutes, covered.

Makes 4-6 servings.

Lamb Riblets Number Two

1 cup **onions,** chopped
1 tablespoon **olive oil**
2 pounds **riblets**

1. In a 2 1/2-quart container, sauté onions in olive oil. Cook 1 minute; stir once.

2. Add riblets. Cook 6 minutes, covered. Turn every 2 minutes.

3. Prepare sauce.

4. Pour sauce over riblets. Cook 19-21 minutes, uncovered. Rearrange and baste every 5 minutes. Rearrange and let stand 5 minutes, covered.

Sauce

1 teaspoon **garlic powder**
2-1/2 tablespoons **white vinegar**
4 tablespoons **lemon juice**
2-1/2 tablespoons **brown sugar**
1 cup **catsup**
1/2 cup **water**
1/2 teaspoon **salt**
1/8 teaspoon **pepper**

In a bowl, combine all ingredients.

Makes 4-6 servings.

Lamb Vegetable Pot

2 pounds **lamb**, cubed
4 tablespoons **olive oil**
1/2 teaspoon **garlic powder**
1 (10-ounce) package frozen **small whole carrots**, thawed
2 (10-ounce) packages frozen **hash brown potatoes**, thawed, crumbled
2 cups **onions**, diced
1 cup **water**
Salt and **pepper**

1. In a 3-quart container, cook meat in olive oil 5 minutes, uncovered. Turn every 60 seconds. Sprinkle with garlic powder.

2. Siphon off excess fat.

3. Layer the meat, carrots, potatoes, and onions. Pour water over the top. Salt and pepper to taste.

4. Cook 16 minutes, covered. Let stand 5 minutes, covered.

Makes 6-8 servings.

Spiced Ground Lamb

1/2 cup **butter**, melted
3 cups **onions**, chopped
2 pounds lean **ground lamb**
2-1/2 teaspoons **ground coriander**
1 tablespoon **turmeric**
1 teaspoon **ground ginger**
1/2 teaspoon **pepper**
8 **cloves**
1 **cinnamon stick**
1 (8-ounce) container **natural yogurt**
1/2 teaspoon **salt**
1 teaspoon **garlic powder**
2 **tomatoes**, chopped
2 cups cooked **rice**
4 tablespoons frozen **chopped chives** or 2 **green onions**, chopped

1. In a 3-quart container, cook onions in butter 3 minutes, uncovered. Stir every 30 seconds.

2. Add the remaining ingredients except rice and chives.

3. Cook 4 minutes, loosely covered with wax paper; stand 2 minutes; stir. Repeat until lamb has cooked 12 minutes. Siphon off excess fat.

4. Serve lamb on top of rice. Garnish with chives or green onions.

Makes 4-8 servings.

Canadian Bacon Casserole

1 (10-ounce) package frozen **Italian beans**
1 (10-ounce) package frozen **cut wax beans**
2 (6-ounce) packages **Canadian bacon**, sliced
1 (10 1/2-ounce) can **cheddar cheese soup**
1/3 cup **sour cream**
1 (15-ounce) can **whole pineapple**, drained

1. Cook Italian and wax beans in packages for 1/2 time. See guide (page 162).

2. In a 2-quart buttered container, place partially cooked beans with Canadian bacon slices over them.

3. In a bowl, combine soup and sour cream. Spoon over beans and bacon.

4. Cook 10-12 minutes, covered. Gently stir soup mixture once.

5. Place pineapple pieces on top of the soup mixture. Cook 3 minutes, covered.

Makes 4-6 servings.

Cheese and Bacon Pudding

16 slices **bread**, crusts cut off, cubed
1/2 cup **bacon**, cooked, crumbled, or precooked **ham** or precooked **shrimp**
1 (10 1/2-ounce) can **cheddar cheese soup**
4 cups **milk**
6 **eggs**, beaten

1. In a 3-quart greased container, layer bread, meat or shrimp, and cheese; end with cheese.

2. In a bowl, mix milk and eggs together; stir. Pour over bread mixture.

3. Cook 7-10 minutes, loosely covered with wax paper. Let stand 10 minutes before serving.

Makes 8 servings.

Ham-Asparagus Rollups

12 slices **ham,** boiled
2 (15-ounce) cans **asparagus** or 2 (10-ounce) packages frozen **asparagus,** thawed
1 (10 1/2-ounce) can **white sauce**
1/4 cup **blue cheese,** crumbled

1. On each slice of ham, lay 3 or 4 asparagus tips; roll up and fasten with toothpicks.

2. Place ham, seam side down, in a rectangular container and pour white sauce over it. Sprinkle with blue cheese.

3. Cook 7-8 minutes, covered. Rotate 1/4 turn every 2 minutes.

Makes 4-6 servings.

Ham Casserole

3 cups **ground ham**
1-3/4 cups **cheddar cheese,** grated
3 **eggs,** beaten
3/4 cup **soda crackers,** crumbled (about 16 crackers)
1 cup **milk**
1 tablespoon **Worcestershire sauce**

1. In a 3-quart container, combine all ingredients.

2. Cook 12-14 minutes, covered. Let stand 5 minutes, covered.

3. Serve with mustard sauce (see page 46).

Makes 4 servings.

NOTE: May also be used as a sandwich filling.

Tahitian Ham Roll

1 pound ground smoked ham
1 pound ground pork
3/4 cup soda crackers, crumbled (about 16 crackers)
2 tablespoons instant minced onion
1/2 cup milk
1 egg, beaten
1 tablespoon dried parsley flakes
Pepper to taste
8 slices canned pineapple

1. Prepare sauce.

2. In a bowl, combine all ingredients except pineapple.

3. Shape into 9 patties about the size of a pineapple slice.

4. In a shallow container, alternate the patties and the pineapple slices in a loaf. Start and end with a pattie, or place inside a plastic bake-in-bag; slit bag. Cook 13-15 minutes. Rotate 1/3 turn every 5 minutes.

5. Pour sauce over ham roll. Cook 4 minutes, uncovered. Baste 3 times during cooking period. Let stand 5 minutes, covered.

Sauce

1/4 cup pineapple syrup
1 cup brown sugar
2 tablespoons vinegar
1 teaspoon prepared mustard

In a bowl, combine all ingredients.

Makes 9 servings.

Link Sausages

8 link sausages

Cook sausages 4-5 minutes between paper towels.

Makes 4 servings.

Pork Sirloin Pie

1 frozen uncooked **loaf of bread,** defrosted
2 cups **onions,** chopped
1 (2-ounce) can **pimentos**
2 tablespoons dried **sweet pepper flakes**
2 tablespoons **garlic powder**
1/2 pound lean **ham** or **sausage**
1/2 cup **vegetable oil**
1/2 pound **pork sirloin,** cut in small cubes
1-1/2 teaspoons **butter**
3 teaspoons **tomato sauce**
3/4 cup **white or red wine**
1/8 teaspoon **powdered saffron**
Salt and **pepper** to taste

1. Roll dough to form an 8 x 16-inch rectangle. Cut in 2 equal square parts.

2. In a 2-quart container, sauté the onions, pimentos, sweet pepper, garlic powder, and ham or sausage in oil. Cook 3 minutes, covered loosely with wax paper. Stir every 3 minutes. (If sausage is used, cook 5 minutes.)

3. Add pork sirloin, butter, tomato sauce, wine, saffron, and salt and pepper. Cook 4 minutes, covered. Stir after 3 minutes. (If leftover pork roast is used, cook 2 minutes.)

4. Place one dough square in a greased 8 x 8 x 2-inch container. Cook 2 minutes, uncovered. On top of this pour the meat filling. Cover filling with the other dough square.

5. Moisten the dough edges and squeeze together. Prick the pastry with fork tine.

6. Cook 6-8 minutes, uncovered. Rotate 1/4 turn every 2 minutes. Brown in microwave oven with browning element or conventionally.

Makes 6 servings.

Corn Stuffing Pork Chops

8 **pork chops** 3/4 inch thick
2-3 tablespoons **vegetable oil**
Pepper to taste

1. Trim excess fat from chops and slice a pocket in the middle of each. Brown in oil conventionally. Season with pepper.

2. Prepare stuffing.

3. Stuff each pork chop pocket with mixture. Fasten with 1 or 2 toothpicks.

4. Place chops in a 7 x 12-inch container or cook in plastic bake-in-bags individually or together. Any leftover dressing can be placed on top of the meat. Cook 25-27 minutes. Rearrange once during cooking period. Let stand 5 minutes, covered.

Stuffing

1 (8 3/4-ounce) can **cream-style corn**
1-1/2 cups fine **bread crumbs** or **cracker crumbs**
3 tablespoons instant **minced onion**
2 tablespoons dried **sweet pepper flakes**
Salt and **pepper** to taste

In a bowl, combine all ingredients.

Makes 8 servings.

Spicy Pork Chops

6 **pork chops** 3/4 inch thick
2 tablespoons **vegetable oil**
1/3 cup dried **bread crumbs**

1. In a 2-quart (7 x 12-inch) container, cook pork chops and oil 5 minutes, covered. Turn once.

2. Prepare sauce.

3. Pour 1/2 the sauce and sprinkle 1/2 the bread crumbs over the pork chops. Cook 10 minutes, covered.

4. Turn chops; pour remaining sauce and sprinkle remaining crumbs over them. Cook 10-12 minutes, uncovered. Let stand 10 minutes, covered.

Sauce

1 (7/8-ounce) envelope **beef gravy mix**
1 (1 1/2-ounce) envelope **spaghetti sauce mix**
1-1/4 teaspoons **chili powder**
3/4 cup **water**

Combine all ingredients.

Makes 6 servings.

Texas Pork Chops

1 teaspoon **seasoned salt**
4 tablespoons **flour**
6 **pork chops**
3 tablespoons **vegetable oil**
2-1/2 cups **water**
1 (8-ounce) can **tomato sauce**
3 tablespoons instant **minced onion**
2 tablespoons dried **sweet pepper flakes**
1-1/2 teaspoons **salt**
1 (1 1/4-ounce) envelope **chili seasoning mix**
1 cup uncooked **rice**

1. In a bowl, mix seasoned salt with flour. Dredge pork chops.

2. Brown pork chops in oil conventionally.

3. In a 2 1/2-quart container, combine water and tomato sauce. Add the minced onion, sweet peppers, salt, and chili seasoning mix; stir.

4. Add rice; stir.

5. Place pork chops on top of rice. Cook 18-20 minutes, covered. Turn meat once during cooking period. Let stand 8 minutes, covered.

Makes 6 servings.

Sausage Biscuit Bake

1-1/3 cups **biscuit mix**
1 cup **sugar**
3 tablespoons **vegetable oil**
1 **egg,** beaten
3/4 cup **buttermilk**
1 teaspoon **vanilla extract**
1/2 teaspoon **nutmeg**
1/4 teaspoon **cinnamon**
1 tablespoon **dried parsley flakes**
1 tablespoon **instant minced onion**
12 **sausages**

1. In a bowl, combine all ingredients except sausages.

2. Place sausages in a 2-quart buttered container. Pour batter over the top. Cook 10-12 minutes, uncovered. Rotate 1/4 turn every 2 minutes. Let stand 5 minutes, uncovered. Invert on a platter. Serve warm.

Makes 6 servings.

Sausage Cake

1 pound **pork sausage**
1 **spice cake mix**
1 cup **brown sugar**
1 teaspoon **ginger**
1 teaspoon **pumpkin pie spice**
1 teaspoon **instant coffee**
1 cup **raisins**
1 cup **walnuts,** chopped
2 **eggs,** beaten
1 cup **water**
1/2 cup **vegetable oil**

1. In a 1-quart container, cook crumbled meat 5 minutes, loosely covered with wax paper. Stir every 30 seconds. Siphon off excess grease.

2. In a bowl, combine all ingredients and pour into a 7 x 12-inch container; cook 10-12 minutes, uncovered. Rotate 1/4 turn every 2 minutes.

Makes 8 servings.

NOTE: Fill container 3/4 full. Use extra batter for cupcakes.

Veal Birds

2 tablespoons **prepared mustard**
6-8 **veal steaks**, cut thin, pounded
1/2 cup **flour**
Salt and **pepper** to taste
2 tablespoons **vegetable oil**
1 cup **tomato juice**

1. Prepare stuffing.
2. Spread mustard over steaks.
3. Place equal portions of stuffing on each steak. Roll up and tie or secure with toothpicks.
4. In a bowl, combine flour, salt, and pepper, and dredge veal birds.
5. In a 9-inch pie plate, heat oil; cook 1 minute 30 seconds, uncovered. Place veal birds in the oil in a circular pattern. Cook 7-9 minutes, uncovered. Turn every 30 seconds.
6. Add tomato juice. Cook 9-11 minutes, covered. Turn every 5 minutes.

Stuffing

1 (6-ounce) package **stuffing**
2 teaspoons dried **orange peel**
1 **egg**, beaten

In a bowl, prepare stuffing according to package directions. Add orange peel and egg.

Makes 8-10 servings.

Veal and Ham in Wine Sauce

3 tablespoons **butter**
8 thin slices **veal**
8 thin slices **prosciutto ham**
1/2 teaspoon **sage**
Pepper to taste
1/2 cup **white wine**
1 (6/10-ounce) envelope **Italian salad dressing mix**

1. In a 7 x 12-inch container, cook butter 30 seconds, uncovered.

2. Secure veal and ham together with toothpicks. (The slices should be about the same size.)

3. Sprinkle meats with sage and pepper and sauté in the butter for 1 minute (30 seconds each side).

4. In a bowl, add wine to salad dressing mix; stir. Pour over meat.

5. Cook 6 minutes 30 seconds, covered, or until veal is tender.

6. Remove toothpicks before serving.

Makes 4 servings.

Veal Loaf

1-1/2 pounds **ground veal**
2 cups **carrots**, grated
2 tablespoons instant **minced onion**
1 (4-ounce) can **mushrooms**, chopped
1 (1 1/2-ounce) envelope **meatloaf seasoning mix**
Salt and **pepper** to taste
1 cup **sour cream**

1. In a bowl, combine all ingredients.

2. In a greased glass loaf pan, cook 12-14 minutes, covered. Invert on a serving dish or plank. Let stand 5 minutes, covered.

Makes 4-6 servings.

Shortcut Veal Oskar

1/2 cup **butter**
8 thin **veal cutlets**
1/3 cup **flour**
1 **egg** beaten with 2-1/2 tablespoons **white wine**
3/4 cup packaged **bread crumbs**
2 (10-ounce) packages frozen cut **broccoli**
1 cup **cheddar cheese soup**, canned
1 (6 1/2-ounce) can **crab meat**, flaked
Paprika

1. In a 7 x 12-inch container, cook butter 1 minute, uncovered.

2. Dredge meat in flour; dip into beaten egg, then bread crumbs. Sauté in butter 1-2 minutes, uncovered.

3. Cook broccoli; see guide (page 162).

4. In a bowl, combine cooked broccoli, 1 cup cheese soup, and crab meat.

5. Place the broccoli mixture on top of each veal cutlet. Sprinkle with paprika.

6. Cook 8-10 minutes, loosely covered with wax paper. Let stand 5 minutes, covered.

7. Brown in the microwave oven with browning element or conventionally.

Makes 6-8 servings.

Italian Veal Pie

1 stick **pie dough mix**
1 teaspoon **garlic powder**
1 teaspoon dried **Italian seasonings**
1/3 cup canned **grated Parmesan cheese**
1/2 cup **cheddar cheese, grated**

1. Prepare filling.

2. In a bowl, prepare pie dough mix according to package directions.

3. Cut seasonings and Parmesan cheese into the pie dough. Add more water if needed.

4. Roll out 3/4 of dough to fit a 9-inch glass pie plate. Roll out rest of dough and cut in 3-inch circles. See Prepare Pastry (page 231).

5. Pour meat filling into pie shell. Top with cheddar cheese and dough circles. Cook 3 minutes, uncovered. Brown in microwave oven with browning element or conventionally.

Filling

1 pound **veal steak**, cut in small pieces
1/2 cup **flour**
1/4 cup **vegetable oil**
1 (15-ounce) can **whole tomatoes**
1 (8-ounce) can **tomato sauce** or 3/4 cup
1/3 cup **onions**, chopped
3 tablespoons canned **grated Parmesan cheese**
3 tablespoons **mozzarella cheese**, grated
1 tablespoon **sugar**
2 teaspoons dried **Italian seasonings**
1/8 teaspoon **salt**
1/8 teaspoon **garlic powder**

1. Dredge the meat in flour.

2. In a 2-quart container, cook meat and oil 5 minutes, covered. Stir every 60 seconds.

3. Add the remaining ingredients. Mix. Cook 15 minutes, covered. Stir every 5 minutes.

Makes 4-6 servings.

Veal and Pork Casserole

1 pound **pork**, cubed
1 pound **veal**, cubed
2 quarts hot **water**
1/8 teaspoon **salt**
1/4 cup **celery**, chopped
2 (7-ounce) packages **noodles**
2 (10 1/2-ounce) cans **cream of chicken soup**
1 (16-ounce) can **cream-style corn**
1/2 cup fine **bread crumbs**

1. In a 3-quart container, cook meats, water, salt, and celery 12 minutes, covered. Remove meat and set aside. Save broth.

2. Cook noodles in the broth (add water if needed). Cook 4 minutes less than time in guide (page 118). Drain; do not rinse.

3. Stir in soup and corn.

4. Add meats and stir. Sprinkle bread crumbs over the top. Cook 7-9 minutes, covered. Let stand 5 minutes, covered.

Makes 6-8 servings.

Pastas: Points to Remember

1. Because pastas have to rehydrate before cooking, you don't save cooking time; but if you follow the directions, they will never scorch.
2. After cooking, drain and rinse.
3. Partially cook noodles when using them in a casserole.

Pasta Guide

Pasta has to rehydrate before cooking. You don't save cooking time.

NAME	AMOUNT	ADDITIONS	DIRECTIONS	TIME
Canelloni; Lasagna Noodles; Linguini; Macaroni; Noodles, Plain or Spinach; Rotini; Shells, Small; Spaghetti, Broken or Long	7-8 oz.	1 teaspoon salt	Fill 3-qt. container 3/4 full of water. Heat water 6-8 min.	
			Add pasta.	7-10 min., uncovered.
			After cooking, drain and rinse.	Stand 3-4 min. covered.
Manicotti	8-10 oz.	1-1/2 teaspoons salt	Fill 4-qt. container 3/4 full of water. Heat water 9-12 min.	
Shells, Jumbo	8-10 oz.			
Spaghetti, Elbow or Rings	10-12 oz.		Add pasta.	9-12 min., uncovered.
Vermicelli, Coiled	10-12 oz.			
			After cooking, drain and rinse.	Stand 3-4 min., covered.

NOTE: Do not allow standing time when pasta is to be used in a casserole.

Macaroni Chipped Beef

2 cups **macaroni**
1 (2 1/2-ounce) jar **chipped beef**
1 (10 1/2-ounce) can **white sauce**
1/2 cup **bread crumbs**
3 tablespoons **butter,** melted

1. Cook macaroni 4 minutes. See guide (page 118). Drain and rinse. Noodles will be limp, but not done.

2. In a 1 1/2-quart buttered container, combine macaroni, beef, and white sauce. Cook 7 minutes, covered. Stir every 2 minutes.

3. Sprinkle bread crumbs and pour melted butter over the top. Cook 2 minutes, uncovered.

Makes 4-6 servings.

Multiple Choice Lasagna

1 pound **curly-edged lasagna noodles**

1/2 cup canned **grated Parmesan cheese**

1. All recipes will use the lasagna noodles, cheese filling, and 1/2 cup canned grated Parmesan cheese.

2. Cook noodles. See guide (page 118).

3. Prepare cheese filling.

4. To assemble, pour a little of the sauce into a 2-quart (7 x 12-inch) container. Cover sauce with a layer of cooked noodles. Over noodles spoon the cheese filling. Pour sauce over cheese filling. Add the second layer of noodles. Layer until all ingredients are used. End with sauce sprinkled with 1/2 cup grated Parmesan cheese.

5. Cook 10-15 minutes, loosely covered with wax paper. Let stand 5 minutes, loosely covered, before serving.

Cheese Filling

1/2 cup canned **grated Parmesan or Romano cheese**
1-1/2 cups **ricotta** or **creamed cottage cheese**
1-1/2 cups **mozzarella cheese,** grated
6 tablespoons dried **parsley flakes**
1/2 teaspoon **pepper**
1 teaspoon **salt** or to taste

In a bowl, combine all ingredients.

Chicken Sauce

2 cups **onions,** chopped
1/2 cup **chicken livers,** chopped
1/4 cup **olive oil**
2 teaspoons **garlic powder**
2-3 cups **chicken,** cooked, chopped
1/3 pound **prosciutto ham,** chopped
1 (2-ounce) can **mushrooms**
2 (15-ounce) can **tomatoes**
1 (12-ounce) can **tomato paste**
1 cup **dry white wine**
1 teaspoon dried **Italian seasonings**
Salt and **pepper** to taste

1. In a 3-quart container, sauté onions and chicken livers in oil 3 minutes. Sprinkle with garlic powder; stir.

2. Add the remaining ingredients; stir. Cook 4 minutes; stir twice during cooking period.

Cream Sauce

2 (10 1/2-ounce) cans **white sauce**
1/2 teaspoon **nutmeg**
8 tablespoons dried **parsley flakes**
2 cups **cream**
2 **eggs,** beaten
Salt and **pepper** to taste

1. In a 3-quart container, combine the white sauce, nutmeg, parsley, salt and pepper, and 1 cup cream; cook 5 minutes, covered.

2. Beat eggs with remaining cream.

3. Whisk egg mixture slowly into the hot white sauce; stir. Cook 3 minutes. Stir every 30 seconds.

Meat Sauce

2 cups **onions,** chopped
2 pounds **ground beef**
1/4 cup **olive oil**
2 teaspoons **garlic powder**
2 (15-ounce) cans **tomatoes**
1 (12-ounce) can **tomato paste**
1 (4-ounce) can **mushrooms**
1/4 teaspoon **cayenne**
1-1/2 tablespoons **sugar**
2 **bay leaves**
1 teaspoon dried **Italian seasonings**
Salt and **pepper** to taste

1. In a 3-quart container, sauté onions and meat in oil. Sprinkle with garlic powder. Cook 8 minutes, loosely covered with wax paper. Stir every 30 seconds for first 5 minutes, then stir every 60 seconds. Siphon off grease.

2. Add the remaining ingredients. Cook 4 minutes, covered. Stir once during cooking period.

Shellfish and Fish Sauce

1 recipe **cream sauce** (See page 120.)
4 cups **shrimp, clams, lobster, scallops,** or **crab**, uncooked, or any **white fish**, cooked, flaked, deboned

1. In a 3-quart container, cook the cream sauce.

2. Add shellfish or fish and stir. Let stand 3-4 minutes, covered. (Do not cook.)

Makes 6-8 servings.

Chinese Casserole

4 (3-ounce) packages chicken-flavored **top ramen noodles**
4 cups **water**
1 (10-ounce) package frozen **Chinese vegetables**, defrosted
1 (10 1/2-ounce) can **tomato bisque soup**
1 (10 1/2-ounce) can **cream of mushroom soup**
1 (6-ounce) can **water chestnuts**, sliced
2 tablespoons **soy sauce**
1 (6-ounce) can **mushrooms**, drained, sliced
1 cup **celery**, chopped
1 cup **chicken**, cooked, diced
4 **green onions and tops**, chopped
1 cup **cashews**, broken
1 (5-ounce) can **chow mein noodles**

1. Combine noodles, water, and seasoning packet in a 3-quart container; cook 2 minutes, covered.

2. Add the remaining ingredients except chow mein noodles; stir.

3. Cook 17-19 minutes, covered. Stir every 5 minutes.

4. Stir in chow mein noodles. Serve immediately.

Makes 8-10 servings.

NOTE: Extra soy sauce may be served with casserole.

Homemade Noodles

1 **egg**
1 cup **flour**
1/2 teaspoon **baking powder**
1/8 teaspoon **salt**

1. In a bowl, combine all ingredients.

2. Roll out dough on a floured board. Make noodles about 1/8 inch thick or thinner.

3. Cut in thin, medium, or wide strips. Let dry 2 hours.

4. Cook 3 minutes longer than guide time for commercially prepared plain noodles. See guide (page 118).

Makes 4-6 servings.

Noodles Español

1 (16-ounce) package **noodles**
2-1/3 cups **onions**, chopped
2 slices **bacon**, cut in 5 pieces each
1 cup **celery**, diced
1/4 cup **olive oil**
2 teaspoons **garlic salt**
1 (15-ounce) can **tomatoes**
2 (4-ounce) cans **mushrooms**
2 tablespoons dried **parsley flakes**
1/2 teaspoon **pepper**
1/2 teaspoon **paprika**
1 **bay leaf**
1/2 teaspoon **oregano**
1 (4-ounce) can **jalapeno chili peppers**, minced
1 teaspoon **powdered cinnamon**
1 **bouillon cube** dissolved in 1 cup **water**
1 (4 1/2-ounce) can **chopped ripe olives**
2 cups **cheddar cheese**, grated

1. Cook noodles 4 minutes. See guide (page 118). Drain and rinse.

2. In a 1-quart container, sauté onions, bacon, and celery in olive oil 4 minutes, uncovered. Stir every 30 seconds. Sprinkle with garlic salt.

3. In a 4-quart container, place noodles and onion mixture. Add the remaining ingredients; stir.

4. Cook 5 minutes, covered. Stir. Cook 7-10 minutes, covered.

Makes 6 servings.

Noodles Neapolitan

1 (8-ounce) package narrow **egg noodles**
1/2 cup **butter**, melted
1/2 cup **onions**, chopped
1 cup **sour cream**
1 cup canned **grated Parmesan cheese**

1. Cook noodles 4 minutes. See guide (page 118). Drain and rinse.

2. In a 2-quart container, cook butter 1 minute, uncovered. Sauté onions in butter 2 minutes, uncovered. Stir every 30 seconds.

3. Add noodles, sour cream, and cheese; stir. Cook 5 minutes, covered. Stir every 60 seconds. Serve immediately.

Makes 4-6 servings.

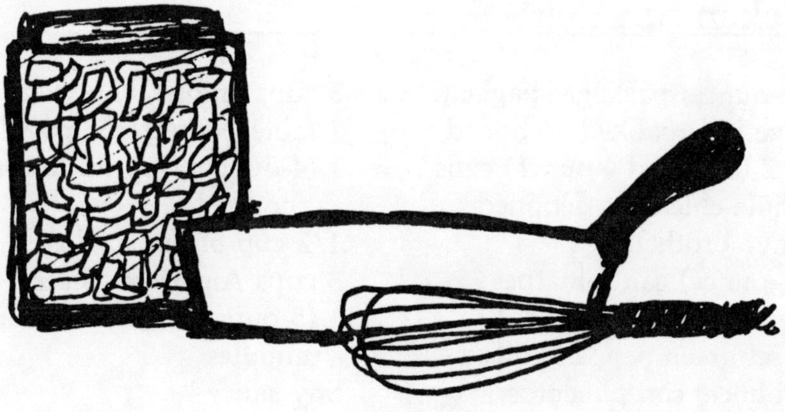

Cheese Noodle Ring

- 1-1/2 cups **egg noodles**
- 1-1/2 cups hot **milk**
- 1-1/4 cups soft **bread crumbs**
- 1/4 cup melted **butter**
- 1 (2-ounce) can chopped **pimentos**
- 2 tablespoons dried **parsley flakes**
- 2 tablespoons instant **minced onion**
- 1-1/2 cups **American cheese,** cubed
- **Salt** and **pepper** to taste
- 1/2 teaspoon **paprika**
- 3 **eggs,** beaten

1. Cook noodles 4 minutes. See guide (page 118). Drain and rinse.

2. In a 2-quart container, heat milk. Cook 1 minute 30 seconds, uncovered.

3. Add bread crumbs, butter, pimentos, parsley, onion, cheese, and seasonings; stir.

4. Add eggs; stir. Fold in noodles.

5. Pour into a greased glass ring mold or a greased 2-quart container.

6. Cook 10 minutes, covered. Let stand 8 minutes, covered. Unmold.

Makes 6 servings.

NOTE: Serve with a creamed vegetable.

Chicken Spaghetti

- 1 (16-ounce) package **spaghetti**
- 1 large **hen,** cooked, deboned, or 2 (3-pound 4-ounce) cans **whole chickens,** deboned (Save broth.)
- 1 (15-ounce) can **tomatoes**
- 1 cup **celery,** diced
- 2 **sweet green peppers,** diced
- 1 (2-ounce) can **pimentos,** chopped
- 3 cups **onions,** chopped
- 1 tablespoon **garlic powder**
- 1 (4-ounce) can **mushrooms,** chopped
- 1/2 cup **butter,** melted
- 3 cups **American cheese,** cubed
- 1 (5-ounce) can **chow mein noodles**
- **Soy sauce**

1. Cook spaghetti 4 minutes. See guide (page 118). Drain and rinse.
2. In a bowl, combine remaining ingredients except chow mein noodles and soy sauce.
3. Mix in spaghetti.
4. Pour into a 4-quart casserole. Cook 17-19 minutes, loosely covered with wax paper. Stir 3 times during cooking period. Let stand 5 minutes, covered.
5. Sprinkle chow mein noodles over the top before serving.
6. Serve soy sauce on the side.

Makes 6-8 servings.

NOTE: The liquid is thinner than conventional Italian spaghetti sauce. This recipe is best prepared up to step 3, refrigerated overnight, and cooked just before serving. Add 7 minutes to cooking time if cold.

Poultry: Points to Remember

1. All poultry cook in the microwave oven. They will be brown with a crispy skin.
2. Always wash poultry before using.
3. Be sure poultry are completely thawed before cooking.
4. Do not fry chicken in the microwave oven. To achieve a fried look and taste, use a crumb coating (see guide, page 127); other coatings can also be used, such as crushed corn flakes or barbecued potato chips.
5. A combination of microwave and conventional cooking can be used on all poultry. Start with microwave and end conventionally except for fried chicken.
6. To speed up cooking time when frying chicken, fry conventionally 12-15 minutes, then place chicken on wax paper in the microwave oven. Arrange pieces in a circular pattern, placing smaller pieces in the center; put giblets in the center tucked under the chicken

pieces. Loosely cover chicken with wax paper. Cook 15 minutes or until done.

7. To speed up cooking time when barbecuing or broiling chicken or Cornish game hen, cook 15 minutes in the microwave oven (see guide, page 126) and then barbecue or broil conventionally about 12-15 minutes or until done.
8. The high point of the breast, the wing tips, and the narrow part of the legs are cooking areas that easily overcook. Cover these areas with foil for the first three-fourths of cooking time to reduce microwave penetration.
9. Do not place meat thermometer in the microwave oven unless it is especially designed for microwave use.
10. To keep meat moist, allow all poultry to stand loosely covered 10-20 minutes before carving.

NOTE: FOLLOW MANUFACTURER'S INSTRUCTIONS FOR THE USE OF ALUMINUM FOIL.

Poultry Guide

Rinse all poultry with cold water before using. Insert meat thermometer into center of breast after the poultry has cooked. DO NOT PLACE MEAT THERMOMETER IN MICROWAVE OVEN.

NAME	AMOUNT	TIME	TEMPERATURE
Roasting Chicken	2-1/2 to 4 lb.	6-7 min. per lb., covered.	180-185°
Duck	2-1/2 to 4 lb.	6-7 min. per lb., covered.	180-185°
Wild Duck	2-1/2 to 3 lb.	5-6 min. per lb., covered.	180-185°
Cornish Hen	1 to 1-1/2 lb.	4 min. 30 sec. to 5 min. per lb., covered.	180-185°
Goose	3 to 5 lb.	5-6 min. per lb., covered.	180-185°

NAME	AMOUNT	TIME	TEMPERATURE
Turkey	10 to 12 lb. or one smaller than cavity size	6-7 min. per lb.	175-180°

1. Baste with butter all over. Salt interior of cavity.
2. Place breast side up in a container near oven cavity size. Place container inside a brown paper bag; roll up end.
3. Replace paper bag twice during cooking period; baste at these times. Siphon off excess juices.

NOTE: The time is approximate. A larger fowl will take slightly longer per pound to cook than a small one.

Poultry Convenience Foods Guide

Boxed

NAME	AMOUNT	DIRECTIONS	MINUTES PER POUND
Chicken Seasoning Coating	2-3/8 oz.	Place seasonings in plastic sack. Place washed, cut-up chicken parts (2-1/2 to 3 lb.) in sack and shake to coat. Place smaller pieces in the center. Cook in 2-qt. container, uncovered. Turn once.	7 min.

Frozen, Thawed

NAME	AMOUNT	DIRECTIONS	MINUTES PER POUND
Baked Breast of Chicken Southern Style	16 oz.	Remove from foil container. Place in 2-qt. container.	9-11 min., covered.
Chicken Chow Mein, Chicken and Dumplings, or Chicken and Noodles	32 oz.	Remove from foil and place in 3-qt. container. Stir twice during cooking period.	12-14 min., covered.
Chicken or Turkey Pie	8-10 oz.	Remove from foil container. Place in bowl about the same size as pie.	6-8 min., covered.

NAME	AMOUNT	DIRECTIONS	MINUTES PER POUND
Creamed Turkey or Chicken	6-1/2 oz.	Remove from foil container. Place in 1-qt. container, covered, or slit pouch. Turn twice.	5-7 min.
Crispy Chicken	16 oz.	Remove from foil container. Place on plate arranged in a circular pattern. Turn once.	9-11 min.
Sliced Turkey and Giblet Gravy	32 oz.	Remove from foil container. Place in 3-qt. container. Stir twice.	12-14 min.
Turkey Roast and Gravy	2 lb. 8 oz. (40 oz.)	Remove from foil container. Place in 3 1/2- to 4-qt. container, covered. Rearrange twice.	14-16 min.
Turkey Tetrazzini	12 oz.	Remove from foil container. Place in 2-qt. container, covered. Stir twice.	6-8 min.

Chicken Livers with Corn Muffins

5 tablespoons **butter**
1 pound **chicken livers,** halved
4 tablespoons instant **minced onion**
1/2 teaspoon dried **Italian seasonings**
1/8 teaspoon **pepper**
3/4 cup **tomato juice**
1 (1 1/8-ounce) envelope **chicken-flavored gravy mix**
1 (10 1/2-ounce) can **condensed cream of mushroom soup**
4 tablespoons dried **parsley flakes**
1 (16-ounce) package **corn muffin mix**

1. In a 2-quart container, cook butter 30 seconds.

2. Sauté chicken livers in butter; cook 3 minutes. Stir every 30 seconds.

3. Add onion, Italian seasonings, pepper, and tomato juice.

4. In a bowl, blend chicken gravy mix into the cream of mushroom soup. Add parsley flakes; stir. Pour over chicken livers.

5. Cook 5 minutes, covered. Stir every 2 minutes. Let stand 3 minutes, covered.

6. Make 6 corn muffins. See guide (page 184). For each serving, pour the chicken liver mixture over a corn muffin.

Makes 4-6 servings.

Almond Chicken Casserole

3 cups **chicken,** cooked, diced
2 cups **celery,** diced
1/2 cup **mayonnaise**
1/2 cup **blue cheese salad dressing**
1 (2 3/4-ounce) package **almonds,** slivered
1 cup **Swiss cheese,** grated
1/2 cup **onions,** chopped
1 (2-ounce) can **pimentos,** chopped
Salt and **pepper** to taste
2 **tomatoes,** cut in wedges

1. In a 2-quart container, combine all ingredients except tomatoes.
2. Cook 10-12 minutes, covered. Stir every 3 minutes.
3. Garnish with tomatoes.

Makes 4-6 servings.

Chinese Oyster Sauce Chicken

1 **chicken,** cut up, or 6 **chicken breasts,** halved
1 cup **oyster sauce,** canned
1 (8-ounce) can **oysters,** drained
1 (10-ounce) package frozen **pea pods,** thawed

1. With a pastry brush, baste chicken pieces with oyster sauce.
2. In a greased 2-quart container, cook chicken 15 minutes, covered.
3. Add oysters; cook 5 minutes, covered.
4. Add pea pods; cook 2 minutes, covered, or until chicken is done.

Makes 4-6 servings.

Chicken in Sour Cream Sauce

4-6 **chicken breasts** or
1 **chicken,** quartered
1/4 cup hot **water**
1 (1 1/2-ounce) package **meat loaf seasoning**
1 cup **sour cream**

1. In a 3-quart container, cook chicken pieces and water 12 minutes, covered. Turn once.

2. In a bowl, combine meat loaf seasoning and sour cream and dredge chicken in the mixture.

3. Return to container and cook 7-10 minutes or until done.

Makes 4-6 servings.

Chicken Versailles

3 **chicken breasts,** skinned, boned, halved (Cut a slit lengthwise in each breast.)
6 thin slices **ham,** cooked
1/3 cup **white wine**
6 thin slices **Swiss cheese**
1 (1 1/2-ounce) package seasoned **shake-n-bake mix**
2 tablespoons dried **parsley flakes**
Salt and **pepper**
1 (2-ounce) can **pimento slices**

1. In a bowl, soak chicken and ham 5 minutes in the wine.

2. Place the ham and cheese in the small cavity of each breast.

3. Sprinkle seasoned coating mixture on a plate. Dredge chicken breasts in mixture.

4. Sprinkle with parsley. Close with 1 or 2 toothpicks.

5. In a 1-quart container, cook 7 minutes per pound, covered.

6. Salt and pepper to taste.

7. Garnish with pimento slices.

Makes 4-6 servings.

Easy Chicken and Rice Casserole

1 cup uncooked **rice**
1 (10 1/2-ounce) can **cream of mushroom soup**
3/4 cup **mayonnaise**
1 cup **celery**, diced
1 tablespoon instant **minced onion**
1 tablespoon **lemon juice**
2 cups **chicken**, cooked
1 (2 3/4-ounce) package **almonds**, slivered
1 cup **cornflakes**, crushed

1. Cook rice 10 minutes. See guide (page 134).

2. In a 2 1/2-quart or 3-quart container, combine all ingredients except almonds and cornflakes.

3. Cook 8 minutes, covered. Stir twice.

4. Sprinkle almonds and cornflakes over the top and cook 2 minutes, uncovered.

Makes 4 servings.

Yodel Chicken

3 tablespoons **flour**
1 teaspoon **salt**
2 tablespoons **paprika**
1/4 teaspoon **celery salt**
6 **chicken breasts**, skinned
3 tablespoons **butter**
1/3 cup **dry sherry**
1 teaspoon **cornstarch**
3/4 cup **whipping cream**
Salt to taste
1/3 cup **sauterne wine**
1 tablespoon **lemon juice**
1/2 cup **Swiss cheese**, grated

1. In a bowl, mix flour, salt, paprika, and celery salt. Dredge chicken breasts until well coated.

2. In a 3-quart container, cook butter 30 seconds, uncovered. Cook chicken pieces in butter for 3 minutes, covered. Turn once.

3. Add sherry and cook, covered, 12-14 minutes. Remove chicken.

4. In a bowl, blend cornstarch with cream and salt. Stir into chicken juices in the container. Cook 1 minute, covered.

5. Add wine and lemon juice. Cook 1 minute, covered. Add chicken; cook 3 minutes, covered.

6. Sprinkle cheese over the top. Brown in microwave oven with browning element or conventionally. Let stand 5 minutes, covered.

Makes 4-6 servings.

Spanish Duck

1/2 cup **vegetable oil**
1 **duck**, quartered
1/2 pound **turnips**, sliced
1-1/2 cups frozen **baby onions,** thawed
1 **bay leaf**
1/8 teaspoon **thyme**
1/8 teaspoon **marjoram**
1 teaspoon **garlic powder**
2 tablespoons dried **parsley flakes**
Salt to taste
1/2 pound **bacon, cut in** squares
1 (10-ounce) package frozen **sliced carrots, thawed**
1-1/2 cups **dry white wine**
1 cup **dry anisette**
1 (1 1/8-ounce) envelope chicken or beef gravy mix
12 chestnuts, peeled (optional)

1. In a 4-quart container, cook oil 1 minute, uncovered. Add the duck and brown each side about 2 minutes.

2. Add turnip, onions, and seasonings; cook 2 minutes, covered.

3. Add bacon; cook 2 minutes, covered.

4. Siphon off excess fat. Add carrots, wine, and anisette; cook 7 minutes, covered.

5. Make gravy mix according to package directions; pour over duck. Add nuts; cook 10 minutes, covered, or until done.

Makes 4 servings.

Cornish Game Hens

2 Cornish **game hens**, halved lengthwise
2 tablespoons **butter**, melted
1/2 teaspoon **garlic salt**
Salt and **pepper** to taste
1/2 cup **sour cream**

1. Sprinkle hen cavities with garlic, salt, and pepper. With a pastry brush, baste hens with butter. Cook 10 minutes, covered. Let stand covered while sauce cooks.

2. Prepare sauce.

3. Pour sauce over the hens and cook 5 minutes, uncovered, or until done.

4. Remove hens from container. Blend sour cream into hot sauce. Pour over hens and serve immediately.

Sauce

5 tablespoons **butter**
1 tablespoon **flour**
4 tablespoons instant **minced onion**
1/2 pound fresh **mushrooms** or 2 (4-ounce) cans **sliced mushrooms**, drained
1/2 cup **dry white wine**
1 (15-ounce) can **tomatoes**, diced, drained

1. In a 1-quart container, cook butter 30 seconds. Stir in flour to make a paste.

2. Add all ingredients. Stir to blend. Cook 3 minutes, covered. Stir every 30 seconds.

Makes 2-4 servings.

NOTE: The hens can be cooked through step 2 several hours before or the day before serving. Reheat 3-5 minutes, then add the flour and sour cream minutes before serving.

Rice: Points to Remember

1. Rice has to rehydrate before cooking. You do not save time, but the microwave method is good to use.
2. All cooked rice reheats nicely. Cover with plastic wrap and cook one to two minutes for each cup.

Rice Guide

Rice has to rehydrate before cooking. You don't save cooking time.

NAME	AMOUNT	ADDITIONS	DIRECTIONS	TIME
White or Brown Rice	1 cup	1 teaspoon butter	Fill 1 1/2-qt. container with 2-1/2 cups water. Add rice.	12-13 min., covered. Stand 5 min., covered.
Quick-Cooking Rice	1-1/2 cups	1 teaspoon salt	Fill 1-qt. container with 1-1/2 cups water. Cook water 2 min. 30 sec. to 3 min. Add quick-cooking rice.	5 min., covered.
Wild Rice, Instant	2 cups		Fill 1 1/2-qt. container with 2 cups water. Add wild rice.	4 min., covered. Stand 5 min., covered.
Wild Rice, Regular	2-3/4 cups	1/2 teaspoon salt	Fill 2-qt. container with 2-3/4 cups water. Add wild rice.	40 min., covered.

Rice Convenience Foods Guide

Boxed

NAME	AMOUNT	DIRECTIONS	TIME
Seasoned White or Brown Rice with or without Vermicelli	1 (6-oz.) pkg.	Prepare according to pkg. directions. Cook in 2 1/2-qt. container. Stir once.	15 min., covered. Stand 5 min., covered.

NAME	AMOUNT	DIRECTIONS	TIME
Seasoned Quick-Cooking Rice with or without Vermicelli	1 (6-oz.) pkg.	Prepare according to pkg. directions. Cook in 2 1/2-qt. container.	3 min., covered. Stand 5 min., covered.
Wild Rice and White Rice Mix	1 (6-oz.) pkg.	Prepare according to pkg. directions. Cook in 2 1/2-qt. container.	15 min., covered. Stand 5 min., covered.

Frozen

NAME	AMOUNT	DIRECTIONS	TIME
Cooked Rice	1 (10-oz.) pkg.	Cook in pouch. Slit bag. Turn once.	5 min.

Chicken Gumbo Rice

2 cups uncooked **rice**
2 (10 1/2-ounce) cans **chicken gumbo soup**
1/4 cup **water**

1. In a 2-quart container, combine all ingredients.
2. Cook 20 minutes, covered.

Makes 4-6 servings.

Chinese Fried Rice

2 (6-ounce) packages **fried rice mix**
2 tablespoons **butter,** melted
1 pound **boneless pork,** cut in very small pieces
1 teaspoon **garlic salt**
1 cup **onions,** chopped
1 (2-ounce) can **mushrooms,** stems and pieces, drained
1 **egg,** beaten
Soy sauce

1. Prepare fried rice according to package directions. See guide (page 134).

2. In a 2-quart container, cook butter 30 seconds, uncovered.

3. Add pork; sprinkle with garlic salt. Cook 5 minutes, loosely covered with wax paper. Stir every 60 seconds.

4. Add onions. Cook 3 minutes, loosely covered.

5. Add mushrooms. Cook 1 minute, loosely covered.

6. Add egg; stir. Cook 1 minute, uncovered. Stir every 20 seconds.

7. Blend cooked rice into meat mixture; cook 2 minutes, covered. Stir every 30 seconds. Add more butter if needed.

8. Serve with soy sauce.

Makes 4-6 servings.

Curry Rice

3 tablespoons **butter**
1 **apple**, peeled and diced
1 cup **onions**, chopped
1 cup uncooked **rice**
1 teaspoon **curry powder**
1/2 teaspoon **saffron**
1/2 cup **chutney**

1. Prepare bouillon broth.

2. In a 2-quart container, cook butter 30 seconds, uncovered.

3. Cook apple and onions in butter 3 minutes, uncovered. Stir every 30 seconds.

4. Add remaining ingredients except chutney.

5. Add bouillon broth to rice mixture. Cook 12-13 minutes, covered.

6. Add chutney to the hot rice; stir. Serve immediately.

Bouillon Broth

2-1/2 cups water
1 bouillon cube

1. In a 1-quart container, cook water 2 minutes 30 seconds, uncovered.

2. Add bouillon cube; stir to dissolve.

Makes 4-6 servings.

Genoa Rice

15 strips **bacon**
1 (6-ounce) package **Italian rice mix**
1 (10-ounce) package **frozen peas**, thawed
1 (4-ounce) can **mushrooms**, drained
1 tablespoon **butter**
1/8 teaspoon **salt**
1 teaspoon **lemon juice**
2 tablespoons dried **sweet pepper flakes**
3 tablespoons dried **parsley flakes**

1. Cook bacon. See guide (page 92). Crumble.
2. In a 2-quart container, prepare rice mix according to package directions. See guide (page 134).
3. Add peas; cook 5 minutes, covered.
4. Add remaining ingredients. Cook 5 minutes, covered.
5. Let stand 5 minutes, covered.

Makes 4-6 servings.

Indonesian Rice

1/2 cup **butter**
1 cup **onions**, diced
3 tablespoons dried **sweet pepper flakes**
1 (6-ounce) package **curried rice mix**
1 cup **chicken**, cooked, diced
1/2 cup **ham**, cooked, diced
1 pound **shrimp**, peeled, deveined, cooked, diced
1 (8-ounce) can **crab meat**, flaked

1. Prepare bouillon broth.
2. In a 3-quart container, cook butter 2 minutes, uncovered.

3. Add onions, pepper flakes, and rice. Sauté 5 minutes, uncovered. Stir every 30 seconds.

4. Add bouillon broth to rice. Cook 2 minutes, covered. Stir once.

5. Add chicken and ham. Cook 17 minutes, covered, or until rice is cooked. Add shrimp; cook 2 minutes, covered.

6. Spread crab meat flakes over the rice. Let stand 5 minutes, covered.

Bouillon Broth

2 cups **water**
2 **bouillon cubes**
Seasoning packet from rice mix

1. In a 1-quart container, heat water. Cook 3 minutes, uncovered.

2. Add bouillon cubes and seasoning packet; stir to dissolve.

Makes 8-9 servings.

Rice Pilaf

4 tablespoons **butter**
1-1/2 cups uncooked **brown rice**
1/2 teaspoon **Accent**
6 tablespoons dried **parsley flakes**
3/4 cup **carrots,** minced
3/4 cup **celery,** minced
1/2 cup **green onions,** chopped, or 1/4 cup dried **shredded green onions**
3/4 cup **pignolia (pine) nuts** or 3/4 cup **almonds,** blanched

1. Prepare bouillon broth.

2. In a 2-quart container, cook butter 30 seconds, uncovered.

3. Add rice. Cook 1 minute 30 seconds, uncovered. Stir every 15 seconds.

4. Add bouillon broth.

5. Add the remaining ingredients except nuts; stir. Cook 15 minutes, covered. Stir twice.

6. Add nuts; stir. Cook 3-5 minutes, covered.

Bouillon Broth

3 cups **water**
3 **bouillon cubes**

1. In a 1-quart container, heat water. Cook 3 minutes, uncovered.
2. Add bouillon cubes; stir to dissolve.

Makes 4-6 servings.

Rice Consommé

1 (10 1/2-ounce) can **consommé**
1/2 cup **water**
1 cup uncooked **rice**
2 tablespoons instant **minced onion**
1 (2-ounce) can **mushrooms**, drained

1. In a 1-quart container, combine all ingredients.
2. Cook 13 minutes, covered.

Makes 4 servings.

Spanish Rice

2 cups **onions**, chopped
1 large **tomato**, diced
2 tablespoons **vegetable oil**
1 cup uncooked **rice**
2-1/2 cups **water**
1/2 teaspoon **chili powder**
1/8 teaspoon **cayenne pepper**
1/2 cup **cheddar cheese**, grated

1. In a 1 1/2-quart container, cook onions and tomato in oil 3 minutes, uncovered. Stir every 30 seconds.
2. Add the remaining ingredients except cheddar cheese. Cook 12-13 minutes, covered. Stir after 10 minutes.

3. Mix cheese into cooked rice mixture. Serve immediately.

Makes 4-6 servings.

Spicy Brown Rice

4 tablespoons **butter**
1-1/2 cups uncooked **brown rice**
1 cup **onions**, chopped
2 tablespoons dried **sweet pepper flakes**
3-3/4 cups **water**
1 (2-ounce) can **mushrooms**, stems and pieces, drained
1/8 teaspoon **salt** and **pepper**
4 drops **Tabasco sauce**
1/4 teaspoon **chili powder**

1. In a 2-quart container, cook butter 30 seconds, uncovered.

2. Add rice, onions, and pepper flakes. Cook 2 minutes, uncovered. Stir every 30 seconds.

3. Add the remaining ingredients. Cook 16 minutes, covered.

Makes 6 servings.

Sandwiches

The Earl of Sandwich is given credit for the invention of the sandwich because he liked to eat while he gambled—his food was served to him between two pieces of bread at the gaming table. However, in France, the custom dates further back to a time when field workers ate meat pressed between two pieces of bread for their noonday meal.

Sandwiches: Points to Remember

1. Always cook or heat sandwiches on paper towels, napkins, or plates. As sandwiches heat, the bread moisture comes to the outside; using paper products allows this moisture to escape.

2. The same sandwich filling cooks in the same amount of time whether cooked open faced or placed between two slices of bread.
3. Frozen bread does not affect cooking time.
4. Do not use frozen filling.
5. If sandwiches are overcooked, the bread will be tough and rubbery.

Sandwich Convenience Foods Guide

Frozen

NAME	AMOUNT	DIRECTIONS	TIME
Corn Dogs	1	Place on paper towel. For more than 1, arrange in a spoke pattern, wooden sticks to outside.	1 min. to 1 min. 30 sec., uncovered. Add 1 min. 15 sec. for each additional corn dog.
English Muffin Halves with Topping	2 halves	Arrange on paper towel in a circular pattern.	2 min. 30 sec. to 3 min., uncovered.
Sandwiches	1 sandwich	Remove wrapping. Place on paper towel. Filling must be thin or bread will overcook.	1 min. 45 sec., uncovered.
Sloppy Joe Sauce with Beef	26 oz. Makes 4-6 sandwiches.	Remove from foil container. Place in 2-qt. container. Stir twice. Spoon hot mixture over warm hamburger buns.	9-10 min.

Hamburger Guide

Room Temperature

AMOUNT	RARE	MEDIUM	WELL-DONE
1 patty	1 min. 30 sec.	2 min.	2 min. 30 sec.
2 patties	2 min. 30 sec.	3 min.	3 min. 30 sec.
3 patties	3 min.	3 min. 30 sec.	4 min.
4 patties	3 min. 30 sec.	4 min.	4 min. 30 sec.
5 patties	4 min. 30 sec.	5 min.	5 min. 30 sec.
6 patties	5 min. 30 sec.	6 min.	6 min. 30 sec.
7 patties	6 min.	6 min. 30 sec.	7 min.
8 patties	6 min. 30 sec.	7 min.	7 min. 30 sec.

Preheat microwave oven grill platter 5 minutes. Place patties on hot grill or in a shallow rectangular container. Cook loosely covered with wax paper. Turn after first 2 minutes. Let stand 4 minutes. Use 1 pound of hamburger for all the hamburger recipes.

Frozen

Let stand 1 minute midway through cooking time.

AMOUNT	RARE	MEDIUM	WELL-DONE
1 patty	2 min. 30 sec.	3 min.	3 min. 30 sec.
2 patties	3 min. 30 sec.	4 min.	4 min. 30 sec.
3 patties	5 min. 30 sec.	6 min.	6 min. 30 sec.
4 patties	7 min. 30 sec.	8 min.	8 min. 30 sec.
5 patties	8 min. 30 sec.	9 min.	9 min. 30 sec.
6 patties	9 min.	9 min. 30 sec.	10 min.
7 patties	9 min. 30 sec.	10 min.	10 min. 30 sec.
8 patties	10 min. 30 sec.	11 min.	11 min. 30 sec.

Barbecue Burger

2 tablespoons instant **minced onion**
2 tablespoons **catsup** or **barbecue sauce** (See page 43.)
1 **egg,** beaten
Salt and **pepper** to taste

1. Combine all ingredients.
2. Add to hamburger meat.

Better Burger

1 (2 3/4- to 3 1/2-ounce) package **Make A Better Burger**

1. Follow package directions.
2. Add to hamburger meat.

Smothered Burger

1 (7/8-ounce) envelope **beef gravy mix**
1 (2-ounce) can **mushrooms,** chopped

In a 1-quart container, make beef gravy mix according to package directions. Add mushrooms. Cook 2 minutes 30 seconds, covered.

Soy Burger

4 tablespoons **soy sauce**
1 teaspoon **garlic powder**
2 tablespoons **white wine**
1/2 cup **green pepper,** chopped

Add all ingredients to hamburger meat.

Frankfurter Guide

1 Hot dog	25-30 sec.
2 Hot dogs	45-50 sec.
3 Hot dogs	1 min. to 1 min. 10 sec.
4 Hot dogs	1 min. 15-20 sec.
5 Hot dogs	1 min. 30-35 sec.
6 Hot dogs	1 min. 45-55 sec.

Place Frankfurter in a hot dog bun. Wrap in napkin or paper towel.

Bacon Wrap

1 **frankfurter**
American cheese
1 **hot dog bun**

Wrap bacon around frankfurter; place a strip of cheese on bun. Cook frankfurter and bun at the same time but separately. Wrap bun in a napkin. Cook frankfurter on a paper towel.

Barbecued

1-1/4 cups **barbecue sauce**
12 **frankfurters**

1. In a 2-quart casserole, cook sauce 3 minutes, covered. (See page 43.)
2. Add whole or cut-up frankfurters. Cook 6 minutes, covered, or until hot. Stir frankfurters 3 times.

Chipped Beef and Cheese Sandwich

1 cup **Gruyère, Emmentaler,** or **Swiss cheese,** grated
2 tablespoons **cream**
8 thin slices **bread, crusts cut off**
1 (5-ounce) jar **chipped beef**
2 **eggs,** beaten
3 tablespoons **butter** or more if needed

1. In a bowl, combine cheese and cream to make a paste. Spread on each piece of bread.

2. Make sandwiches with chipped beef.

3. Dip each sandwich into beaten egg. In a 7 x 12-inch container, melt butter. Spread evenly over bottom of container. Sauté each side in hot butter about 2 minutes. Brown in microwave oven with browning element or conventionally.

4. Prepare sauce.

5. Pour sauce over sandwiches.

Sauce

1-1/2 tablespoons **butter**
1-1/2 teaspoons **flour**
1 cup **half and half**
2 tablespoons **Swiss cheese,** grated
Pepper to taste

1. Cook butter 20 seconds, uncovered.

2. Blend flour into butter. Stir in half and half gradually.

3. Add cheese; stir.

4. Cook 3 minutes, covered. Stir every 30 seconds.

Makes 4-5 sandwiches.

Monte Cristo Sandwich

8 slices **white bread,** crusts cut off
4 slices **turkey,** cooked
4 slices **American cheese**
4 slices **ham,** cooked
6 tablespoons **butter,** melted
1/2 cup **milk**
1/4 cup **flour**
3 **eggs,** beaten
Salt and **pepper** to taste
1 teaspoon **sugar**
3/4 cup **powdered sugar**
Strawberry jam or **orange marmalade**

1. Make 4 sandwiches by layering the turkey, cheese, and ham in that order. Cut in half; secure each half with toothpicks.

2. Melt butter in a 7 x 12-inch container; cook 1 minute, uncovered. Spread butter evenly over bottom of container.

3. In a bowl, make a batter of the milk, flour, eggs, salt, pepper, and sugar. (Add the flour to the milk first.)

4. Dip each sandwich half into the egg batter and place in the buttered container. Spoon a little butter over the top. Cook 3 minutes, uncovered. Turn; cook 3 minutes, uncovered.

5. Dredge each sandwich in powdered sugar.

6. Serve with jam or marmalade.

Makes 4 sandwiches.

Sandwich Fillings

All these fillings are good on an English Muffin. For best results, very *lightly* toast the muffin and then top with filling. Place on a paper towel. Cook 2-3 minutes, covered loosely with wax paper. Any other bread may be substituted.

Avocado and Chicken

1-1/2 cups **chicken or turkey**
1/2 cup **avocado**, peeled, cubed
2 strips **bacon**, cooked, crumbled
6 slices **American cheese**

1. Combine chicken, avocado, and bacon.

2. Top with cheese.

Makes 6 sandwiches.

Crunchy Cream Cheese

6 teaspoons **cream cheese**
2 teaspoons **Roquefort cheese**

Combine all ingredients.

Makes 2 sandwiches.

Ham and Sweetbreads

3/4 cup **sweetbreads,** cooked, sliced thin
4 tablespoons **butter**
3/4 cup **ham,** cubed
1 recipe **cheese sauce**

1. In a 1-quart container, cook sweetbreads in butter 4 minutes, uncovered. Stir every 30 seconds.
2. Combine with ham.
3. Top with cheese sauce. (See page 43.)

Makes 4-6 sandwiches.

Honey and Pecans

1/2 cup **honey**
2 tablespoons **lemon juice**
1/2 cup **pecans,** chopped

Combine all ingredients.

Makes 4-6 sandwiches.

Indian Cheese

1 (8-ounce) package **cream cheese**
1 teaspoon dried **orange peel**
1 tablespoon **candied ginger,** chopped

Combine all ingredients.

Makes 4-6 sandwiches.

Italian Pizza

1 cup **ground beef,** cooked
1 (10 1/2-ounce) can **pizza sauce** (just enough to moisten beef)
1 teaspoon dried **Italian seasonings mix**
1/2 cup **mozzarella cheese,** shredded

1. In a 1-quart container, cook beef 6 minutes, uncovered. Stir every 60 seconds.

2. Combine all ingredients.

Makes 6-8 sandwiches.

Liver and Bacon

1/2 cup **chicken livers,** cooked, minced
2 tablespoons **butter,** melted
8 strips **bacon,** cooked, crumbled
1 (2-ounce) can **minced mushrooms,** drained
1/2 cup **mayonnaise**

1. In a 1/2-quart container, cook chicken livers 3 minutes, uncovered. Stir every 30 seconds.

2. Combine all ingredients.

Makes 4-6 sandwiches.

Liverwurst

1 (4 3/4-ounce) can **liverwurst**
1/4 cup **chili sauce**
4 tablespoons **mayonnaise**

Combine all ingredients.

Makes 6-8 sandwiches.

Minted Lamb

1-3/4 cups **lamb,** cooked, cold, chopped
4 teaspoons dried **mint leaves** or 2 tablespoons **mint sauce**
1/4 cup **mayonnaise**

Combine all ingredients. Let stand 5 minutes before cooking.

Makes 6-8 sandwiches.

Peanut

1 (8-ounce) package **cream cheese**
1 cup **salted peanuts**, chopped
4 tablespoons dried **parsley flakes**
1/4 cup **carrots**, grated (optional)

Combine all ingredients.

Makes 6-8 sandwiches.

Salmon

1/2 cup instant **potato flakes**
1 (7 1/2-ounce) can **salmon**
Salt and **pepper** to taste
1/4 cup **cucumber**, chopped
1/2 teaspoon **red pepper flakes** or to taste
1 tablespoon **lemon juice**
1/4 cup **green pepper**, chopped

1. Mix potatoes according to package directions.
2. Add the remaining ingredients.

Makes 6-8 sandwiches.

Shellfish

1 (6 1/2-ounce) can **lobster, shrimp,** or **crab meat**, drained
3 **eggs**, hard cooked, chopped fine
1/2 cup **cheddar cheese**, grated
1 teaspoon **Worcestershire sauce**
1 teaspoon **prepared horseradish sauce**
1/4 cup **celery**, minced

Combine all ingredients.

Makes 6-8 sandwiches.

Spinach and Eggs

1/2 (10-ounce) package frozen **chopped spinach**, thawed, drained
4 **eggs**, hard cooked, chopped fine
1/4 cup **celery**, minced
2 tablespoons instant **minced onion**
Salt and **pepper** to taste
1/2 cup **mayonnaise**

Combine all ingredients.

Makes 6 sandwiches.

Tuna Melt

1 (6 1/2-ounce) can **tuna fish**
1/4 cup **celery**, minced
1/2 cup **cheddar cheese**, grated
1/2 cup **mayonnaise**

Combine all ingredients.

Makes 6 sandwiches.

Shellfish: Points to Remember

1. Most shellfish can be exchanged in recipes.
2. Small pieces of frozen shellfish can be cooked frozen.
3. In most recipes, if shellfish are fresh or thawed, use minimum cooking time; if frozen, use maximum cooking time.
4. Canned whole clams can be substituted for oysters in most recipes.
5. Steamed clams are fresh clams cooked in a small amount of water the microwave method. See clams (page 151).
6. Shrimp have a tendency to overcook, so add them at end of cooking time in most recipes.
7. If shellfish are at room temperature, cook one minute less than times given.

Shellfish Guide

NAME	AMOUNT	DIRECTIONS	TIME
Clams	6 in shell	In 2-qt. container, boil 1/4 cup water.	45-50 sec., uncovered.
		Add clams.	3 min., covered. Stand 1-2 min., covered.
		Clam meat should be firm. If not, cook.	30 sec., covered.
Crab	1-1/2 lb. live	In a 3-qt. container, boil 1/2 cup water with 1/2 teaspoon salt.	1 min. 30 sec., uncovered.
		Add crab and cover with second 2- or 3-qt. container.	9 min., covered. Stand 2 min., covered.
		Pry off shell when cooked. If meat is translucent, brush with butter and cook.	30-45 sec., covered.
Crab Meat or Oysters	8 oz.	Wash and clean shellfish.	
		In a glass pie plate, add to 3 tablespoons melted butter. Turn once.	About 6 min., uncovered.
Oysters	6 in shell	Wash thoroughly.	
		In 2-qt. container, boil 1/4 cup water.	45-50 sec., uncovered.
		Add oysters.	3 min., covered. Stand 1-2 min., covered.
		Oyster meat should be firm. If not, cook.	30 sec., covered.
Scallops	8 oz.	As for crab meat.	About 6 min., uncovered.
Shrimp	8 oz.	As for crab meat.	About 4 min., uncovered.

NAME	AMOUNT	DIRECTIONS	TIME
Lobster	2 tails about 8 oz. each	Split hard top shell and expose meat on top.	30 sec.
		Brush with melted butter. Place in shallow container.	2-3 min., covered.
Lobster	1-1/2 lb. live, pegged	In 12 x 7-inch container, boil 1/2 cup water with 1/2 teaspoon salt.	1 min. 30 sec., uncovered.
		Add lobster and cover with second 12 x 7-inch container.	9 min., covered. Stand 2 min., covered.
		Split tail. If meat is translucent in center, brush with melted butter and cook.	30-45 sec., covered.
		Serve with melted or drawn butter.	

Shellfish Convenience Foods Guide

Frozen

NAME	AMOUNT	DIRECTIONS	TIME
Fried Clams	5 oz.	Place on a paper towel. Rearrange after first 30 sec.	1 min.
Lobster Newburg	10 oz.	Slit pouch. Turn twice.	4-5 min.
Oysters	12 oz.	Melt 3 tablespoons butter in glass pie plate, uncovered.	30 sec.
		Add oysters. Turn once.	7 min.
Shrimp or Scallops, Breaded	7 oz.	Place on a paper towel in a circular pattern.	1 min. 30 sec., uncovered.

NAME	AMOUNT	DIRECTIONS	TIME
Shrimp or Scallops, Unbreaded	7 oz.	Place in shallow container in a circular pattern.	1 min. 30 sec.

Crab Casserole

1 cup **brown rice**
2 (7-ounce) cans **crab meat**
5 **eggs**, hard cooked, chopped fine
1-1/2 cups **mayonnaise**
2 tablespoons dried **parsley flakes**
4 tablespoons instant **minced onion**
1 (6-ounce) can **evaporated milk**
Salt and **pepper** to taste
1 cup **cheddar cheese**, grated

1. Cook rice. See guide (page 134).
2. In a 2-quart container, combine rice, crab meat, and eggs.
3. In a bowl, blend together remaining ingredients except cheese. Add to rice mixture; cook 7 minutes, covered.
4. Add cheese. Cook 1 minute, covered.

Makes 4-6 servings.

Crab and Broccoli Casserole

2 (10-ounce) packages frozen **broccoli**, thawed
1 (6 1/2-ounce) can **crab meat** or **tuna**
2 (10 1/2-ounce) cans **cream of celery soup**
1/2 (6-ounce) package **stuffing mix**
1/2 cup **water**
1 cup **cheddar cheese**, shredded

1. In a 2-quart container, cover broccoli with crab meat or tuna.

2. Pour one can of cream of celery soup over mixture.

3. In a bowl, mix stuffing with water to moisten and cover crab mixture.

4. Pour the second can of cream of celery soup over the stuffing.

5. Cook 9-10 minutes, covered. Rotate 1/4 turn every 2 minutes.

6. Sprinkle with cheese; cook 30 seconds, uncovered.

Makes 4-6 servings.

Crab, Lobster, or Salmon Newburg

2 (6 1/2-ounce) cans or 2 (6-ounce) boxes frozen **crab meat, lobster**, or **salmon**, defrosted
4 tablespoons **butter**, melted
2 tablespoons **sherry**
2-4 **egg yolks**
1 cup **half and half** or **evaporated milk**
1/8 teaspoon **salt**
1/8 teaspoon **pepper**
1/8 teaspoon **nutmeg**
1/8 teaspoon **paprika**
4 slices toasted **bread** or 1 cup cooked **rice** or 4 **patty shells**

1. In a 2-quart container, cook crab meat in melted butter 1 minute, uncovered.

2. Add sherry; cook 30 seconds, covered.

3. In a bowl, combine egg yolks, half and half, and seasonings. Add to shellfish. Cook 2-3 minutes, covered. Stir every 30 seconds. (Mixture should be slightly thick.) Let stand 2 minutes, covered.

4. Pour over toast or rice or into a patty shell.

Makes 4 servings.

Oyster-Sausage Pie

1 pound **sausage links**
2 cups dry **biscuit mix**
1/4 cup **corn meal**
2 (8-ounce) cans **oysters** drained (Save juice.)

1. Between paper towels, cook sausages 2 minutes 30 seconds until almost done. Turn often.

2. Combine biscuit mix and corn meal. Add 3/4 cup liquid. (Use all the oyster liquid plus water.)

3. Lay oysters in the bottom of a greased 9-inch pie plate. Pour biscuit mixture over the top. Press in sausages until all are covered.

4. Cook 10-12 minutes, uncovered. Rotate loaf pan 1/4 turn every 2 minutes.

Makes 6-8 servings.

Scallops in the Shell

30 **scallops**
2 tablespoons **butter**, melted
1 (1 1/2-ounce) envelope **cheese sauce mix**
1 (7/8-ounce) envelope **chicken gravy mix**
1/4 cup **white wine**
3/4 cup fine **bread crumbs**
6 **scallop shells** (optional)

1. In a 1-quart container, cook scallops in butter 2 minutes, uncovered. Stir every 30 seconds.

2. Mix cheese sauce and gravy mix according to package directions except use wine for part of liquid; blend until smooth. Cook 4 minutes, uncovered. Stir once during cooking period.

3. Roll scallops in bread crumbs and place 5 in each shell.

4. Pour a portion of sauce over each scallop shell and cover with remaining bread crumbs.

5. Arrange in circular pattern. Cook 4-6 minutes, loosely covered with wax paper.

6. Brown in the microwave oven with browning element or conventionally.

Makes 6 servings.

NOTE: Use other sauces of your choice. Cook either in the scallop shells or in small casserole dishes.

Shellfish Supreme

2 (6 1/2-ounce) cans or 2 (6-ounce) boxes frozen **crab meat**, thawed, flaked
2 (6-ounce) boxes frozen **lobster**, thawed
8 ounces frozen **scallops**, thawed
8 ounces **shrimp**, cooked, peeled, cleaned
1 (10 1/2-ounce) can **shrimp soup**
1 (10 1/2-ounce) can **cream of mushroom soup**
3/4 cup **cream**
3 tablespoons **sherry**
1/8 teaspoon **salt**
1/8 teaspoon **pepper**

1. Prepare topping.

2. In a 3-quart container, combine all ingredients except topping. Cook 9-11 minutes, covered. Stir every 2 minutes.

3. Sprinkle topping over mixture. Cook 1 minute, uncovered.

4. Brown in the microwave oven with browning element or conventionally.

Topping

3 tablespoons fine **bread crumbs**
1/3 cup canned **grated Parmesan cheese**
4 tablespoons dried **parsley flakes**
1/8 teaspoon **paprika**
4 tablespoons **butter**, melted

In a bowl, combine all ingredients.

Makes 8-10 servings.

Shellfish Risotto

1 cup **onions**, chopped
4 tablespoons **butter**
1 cup uncooked **rice**
3 cups **hot chicken broth** (Use 3 bouillon cubes in 3 cups of hot water.)
1/2 teaspoon **salt**
1 (8-ounce) can **minced clams**
3 cups **shrimp**, cooked, peeled, cleaned
1/3 cup canned **grated Parmesan cheese**
3 tablespoons dried **parsley flakes**

1. In a 3-quart container, cook onions in butter 1 minute, uncovered.

2. Add rice, chicken broth, and salt. Cook covered for 7 minutes.

3. Add clams. Cook 7-8 minutes, covered. Add shrimp. Cook 2 minutes, covered.

4. Fluff rice mixture and add cheese and parsley. Let stand 5 minutes, covered.

Makes 4-6 servings.

Easy Indian Shrimp Casserole

1 (10 1/2-ounce) can **shrimp soup**
1/2 cup **white wine**
2 tablespoons **butter**
1/2 teaspoon **curry powder** or more to taste
1/4 cup **chutney**, minced (optional)
2 pounds **shrimp**, peeled, cleaned

1. In a 2-quart container, combine all ingredients except shrimp.

2. Cook 4-5 minutes, covered, or until bubbly.

3. Add shrimp; cook 6-8 minutes, covered. Let stand 5 minutes, covered.

Makes 4 servings.

NOTE: This recipe is good over rice.

Madras Shrimp Sauce

1/3 cup **olive oil**
2 cups **onions**, chopped
1 cup **pepper**, chopped
1/2 cup **celery**, chopped
1 (15-ounce) can **whole tomatoes**
1 (15-ounce) can **tomato puree**
1/4 teaspoon **cayenne**
1/2 teaspoon **garlic salt**
2 **bay leaves**
1 cup **chicken stock** or **bouillon**
Salt and **pepper** to taste
2 tablespoons **curry powder**
3 pounds **shrimp**, peeled, cleaned

1. In a 3-quart container, heat oil 1 minute 30 seconds, uncovered.

2. Add onions, pepper, and celery and cook 3 minutes, uncovered. Stir every 30 seconds.

3. Add the remaining ingredients except curry powder and shrimp; cook 4 minutes, covered.

4. Add curry powder; stir. Cook 1 minute, covered.

5. Add shrimp; cook 7-9 minutes, covered. Let stand 5 minutes, covered.

6. Serve over rice. See page 134.

Makes 6-8 servings.

Skewered Shrimp or Scampi

24 raw **jumbo shrimp** or **scampi**, peeled, cleaned
24 wafer thin slices of **prosciutto ham**
6 bamboo skewers

1. Prepare sauce.
2. Wrap prosciutto around the shrimp.
3. Dip shrimp into the hot sauce and skewer.
4. On wax paper, arrange shrimp in a spoke pattern. Cook 2-3 minutes, uncovered. Turn once.
5. Serve with additional hot sauce for dipping.

Sauce

1 cup **honey**
4 tablespoons **horseradish**
1/2 cup **consommé**
1/8 teaspoon **cayenne pepper**
Salt and **pepper** to taste

In a 1-quart container, combine all ingredients. Cook 4 minutes, uncovered. Stir every 30 seconds.

Makes 6 servings.

VEGETABLES

Someone once suggested that the most enjoyable way to follow a vegetable diet is to let the cow eat it and take yours in roast beef. Thank heavens the cave man didn't believe that! He complained of meat, meat, meat and wailed for something else to eat—he didn't know what. Finally, in desperation, he found some leaves and roots—and vegetables got their start.

People moved into houses and vegetables progressed to a place of importance. Many were believed to have marvelous aphrodisiac qualities, and all kinds of mysterious lore began to surround them. Even their meaning in Latin is "to be active and lively."

Any edible part of a plant belongs to the vegetable kingdom. In some, such as carrots and potatoes, we eat the *root bulbs* or *tubers*. Young asparagus *shoots* are mouth watering. The *leaves* in spinach and the *flowers* in cauliflower and artichokes also please our palate. We devour with relish both ripe (cereal) and green (green peas) *seeds*. Others, like the tomato and cucumber, we think of as vegetables, but they are, in fact, the fruits of the plant.

My creative cooking ability was put to the test the summer my college-age sister Debra became a vegetarian and visited us with six friends. They camped at our place for about three weeks, and white-robed women and turbaned young men introduced me to fantastic new vegetable recipes. The vegetables cooked in the microwave oven held their fresh bright colors, and, more importantly, they tasted better because the nutrients were saved.

Vegetables: Points to Remember

1. Sprinkle salt and other seasonings on the bottom of the pan to keep the vegetable from drying out, or add near the end of the cooking time.
2. Add one to three tablespoons water, cream, or butter to fresh vegetables.
3. Vegetables cook best when covered.
4. Always prick vegetables that come in their own shell, such as potatoes, to allow steam to escape; otherwise, they will explode.
5. Always slit the plastic pouch in which some frozen vegetables are packaged; otherwise, they, too, will explode.
6. Some vegetables can be wrapped in clear plastic or merely placed on paper toweling.
7. Vegetables will be a little firm when removed from the microwave oven, but they will continue to cook for a few minutes.
8. When you combine vegetables, use either all frozen or all canned ones that have similar cooking times.
9. Canned foods need only to be heated; they are already cooked. The liquid can be drained or left in. Cook covered.
10. Thaw frozen vegetables in the carton first when using in a casserole: Remove outer waxed paper. Cook on defrost or cook one minute then stand one minute until the vegetable cooks three minutes or until thawed.
11. Cook frozen vegetables in the carton after having removed the outer waxed paper. Stir or rearrange when they are about half done.
12. An eight- to ten-ounce package of frozen vegetables equals about one and one-half cups.
13. Two packages of frozen vegetables take about 10-13 minutes to cook.

Vegetable Guide

	AMOUNT	TIME
Fresh	4-6 servings	6-9 min.
Frozen	1 (10-oz.) pkg. 2 (10-oz.) pkg.	6-9 min. 10-13 min.
Canned	No. 1 or 202 can 1 cup	4 min. 2 min.

VEGETABLE	AMOUNT	UTENSIL	METHOD	STIR AND REARRANGE	TIME
Artichokes					
Fresh	1	deep container or plastic wrap	1 inch water in container unless in plastic wrap	none	4 min. to 4 min. 30 sec.
Frozen, Hearts	10-oz. pkg.	1-qt., covered.	2 tablespoons water	once	4-5 min.
Asparagus					
Fresh	3/4-1 lb.	rectangular container, covered	1/4 cup water	once	4-6 min.
Frozen, Spears	10-oz. pkg.	1-qt., covered	ice side up	once	7-8 min.
Frozen, Cut	9 oz.	1-qt., covered	1/3 cup water unless in pouch	twice	5-6 min.
Beans, Green or Wax, French or Cut					
Fresh	1 lb.	1 1/2-qt., covered	1/3 cup water	once	10-12 min.
Frozen	10-oz. pkg.	1-qt., covered	3 tablespoons water, ice side up	once	6-7 min.

VEGETABLE	AMOUNT	UTENSIL	METHOD	STIR AND REARRANGE	TIME
Beans, Lima					
Fresh	1 lb.	1-qt., covered	1/2 cup water	once	8-10 min.
Frozen	10-oz. pkg.	1-qt., covered	1/2 cup water	once	8-10 min.
	10-oz. pouch		slit pouch	once	6-7 min.
Beets					
Fresh	4-5 medium	2-qt., covered	covered with water	none	12-16 min.
Broccoli					
Fresh	1-1/2 lbs.	2-qt., covered; stems toward outside of dish; stems slit to the flower	1/4 cup water	none	7-9 min.
Frozen	10-oz. pkg.	1-qt., covered	ice side up	once	8-9 min.
	10-oz. pouch		slit pouch	once	5-7 min.
Brussels Sprouts					
Fresh	1/2 lb.	1-qt., covered	2 tablespoons water	once	4-5 min.
Frozen	10-oz. pkg.	1-qt., covered	2 tablespoons water	once	8-9 min.
	10-oz. pouch		slit pouch	once	5-6 min.
Cabbages					
Fresh	1/2 head	1 1/2-qt., covered	2 tablespoons water	once	5-7 min.
Carrots					
Fresh	2 whole	1-qt., covered	3/4 cup water	once	4-5 min.
Sliced	4 medium	1-qt., covered	2 tablespoons water	once	6-8 min.
Diced	4 medium	1-qt., covered	2 tablespoons water	once	4-6 min.
Frozen	10-oz. pkg.	1-qt., covered	ice side up	once	7-8 min.
	10-oz. pouch		slit pouch	once	6-8 min.

VEGETABLE	AMOUNT	UTENSIL	METHOD	STIR AND REARRANGE	TIME
Cauliflower					
Fresh	1 medium head whole	1 1/2-qt., covered	2 tablespoons water	once	6-8 min.
	1 medium head flowerettes	1 1/2-qt., covered	2 tablespoons water	once	6-8 min.
Frozen	10-oz. pkg.	1-qt., covered	ice side up	once	7-9 min.
	10-oz. pouch	1-qt., covered	slit pouch	once	6-8 min.
Celery					
Fresh	4 cups	1 1/2-qt., covered	2 tablespoons water	once	8-11 min.
Corn on the Cob					
Fresh	1 ear	in husks, casserole, or wax paper	butter, lime juice	none	1 min. 30 sec. to 2 min. 30 sec.
	2 ears			none	3-4 min.
	3 ears			none	3-6 min.
	4 ears			none	6-7 min.
	6 ears			none	8-9 min.
Frozen	2 ears	covered container	no water	none	6-8 min.
	4 ears	covered container	no water	none	10-12 min.
Corn					
Fresh	3 ears	1-qt., covered	3 tablespoons water	once	5-6 min.
Frozen	10-oz. pkg.	1-qt., covered	2 tablespoons water	once	5-6 min.
Eggplants					
Fresh	1 medium	on wax paper	pierce skin	none	10 min.
Onions					
Fresh	1 lb.	1 1/2-qt, covered	no water or 2 tablespoons	none	7 min.

VEGETABLE	AMOUNT	UTENSIL	METHOD	STIR AND REARRANGE	TIME
Onions, in Cream Sauce					
Frozen	10-oz. pkg.	1-qt., covered	no water	once	5-7 min.
Parsnips, quartered, cored					
Fresh	4 medium	1 1/2-qt., covered	1/4 cup water	once	7-9 min.
Peas, Green, Shelled					
Fresh	2 lb.	1-qt., covered	2 tablespoons water	once	6-8 min.
Frozen	10-oz. pkg.	1-qt., covered	ice side up	once	5-7 min.
Peas and Carrots					
Frozen	10-oz. pkg.	1-qt., covered	ice side up	once	6-7 min.
Peas, Black-eyed					
Frozen	10-oz. pkg.	1-qt., covered	1/4 cup water or bacon drippings	once	10-11 min.
Pea Pods					
Frozen	6-oz. pouch	1-qt., covered	slit pouch	once	2-3 min.
Potatoes, Baked					
Fresh	1 medium	on wax paper	pierced skin	none	3 min. 30 sec. to 4 min.
	2 medium		pierced skin; 1-inch space between in oven	none	6 min. 30 sec.
	3 medium		pierced skin; 1 inch apart in oven	none	8 min. 30 sec. to 9 min.
	4 medium		pierced skin; 1 inch apart in oven	none	10-11 min.

VEGETABLE	AMOUNT	UTENSIL	METHOD	STIR AND REARRANGE	TIME
	5 medium		pierced skin; placed in circular pattern; 1 inch apart in oven	none	13-14 min.
	6 medium			none	15-16 min.
	7 medium			none	18-19 min.
	8 medium			none	21-22 min.
Potatoes, Boiled, Quartered					
Fresh	2 medium	1 1/2-qt., covered	covered with salted water	none	8-10 min.
Frozen	10 1/2-oz. pkg.	1-qt., covered	ice side up	once	6-7 min.
Sweet Potatoes (Yams)					
Fresh	1 medium	on wax paper	pierced skin	none	3-4 min.
	2 medium	on wax paper	pierced skin; 1-inch space between in oven	none	5-6 min.
	4 medium	on wax paper	pierced skin; 1 inch apart in oven	none	7-9 min.
	6 medium	on wax paper	pierced skin; placed in circular pattern; 1 inch apart in oven	none	9-11 min.
Spinach					
Fresh	1 lb. or 2 bunches	2-qt., covered	in the water that clings to leaves	twice	5-7 min.
Frozen	10-oz. pkg.	1-qt., covered	ice side up	once	6-7 min.
Squash, Acorn					
Fresh	1 medium	on wax paper	cooked whole; halved; seeds removed	none	6-8 min.
	2 medium			none	12-14 min.

VEGETABLE	AMOUNT	UTENSIL	METHOD	STIR AND REARRANGE	TIME
Squash, Hubbard					
Fresh	6 x 6-inch piece	wrapped in wax paper or in 3-qt., covered	1 inch water in container	none	7-8 min.
Frozen	10-oz. pkg.	1-qt., covered	1 teaspoon butter	twice	6-8 min.
Squash, Zucchini					
Fresh	2 medium	1-qt., covered	1/4 cup water	once	6-7 min.
Frozen	10-oz. pkg.	1-qt., covered	ice side up	once	5-6 min.
Turnips, Sliced					
Fresh	4 medium	1 1/2-qt., covered	1/4 cup water	none	10-12 min.

Vegetable Convenience Foods Guide

Boxed

NAME	AMOUNT	DIRECTIONS	TIME
Potato Flakes	5-1/2 oz.	Prepare according to pkg. directions. In 3-qt. container, place potato flakes. Do not stir.	2 min. to 3 min. 15 sec., covered.
Potato Mix			
Au Gratin, Creamed, Hash Brown, Julienne, or Scalloped	5-1/2 oz.	Prepare according to pkg. directions. In 3-qt. container, place potato mix. Stir 3 times.	14-16 min., uncovered.

Canned

NAME	AMOUNT	DIRECTIONS	TIME
No. 1 Flat	8 oz.	Drain part of liquid. In 1/2-qt. container, place vegetable; add seasoning.	2 min., covered.

NAME	AMOUNT	DIRECTIONS	TIME
303 or No. 1 (regular size for most vegetables)	15-17 oz.	Drain part of liquid. In 1/2-qt. container, place vegetable; add seasoning.	4 min., covered.
No. 2	17-21 oz.	In 1-qt. container, place vegetable; add seasoning.	5-1/2 min., covered.

Frozen

NAME	AMOUNT	DIRECTIONS	TIME
Artichoke Hearts Au Gratin	10 oz.	Slit plastic pouch. Turn once.	4-5 min.
Broccoli Au Gratin	10 oz.	Remove from foil. Place in 2-qt. container. Stir twice.	5-7 min., covered.
Cauliflower Au Gratin	10 oz.	Remove from foil. Place in 2-qt. container. Stir twice.	7-9 min., covered.
Corn Soufflé	12 oz.	Remove from foil. Place in 2-qt. container. Don't stir.	6 min. 30 sec. to 8 min., covered.
Buttered Fried Onion Rings	16-oz. pkg. (8 rings)	Place on a paper towel.	2 min., uncovered.
Baked Stuffed Potato	2 halves	Place on paper plate.	7-8 min., loosely covered with wax paper.
French Fried Potatoes	16 oz.	Place on a paper towel.	9-11 min. uncovered.
Hash Brown Potatoes	12 oz.	Remove from container. Place on paper towel.	7-9 min., loosely covered with paper towel.
Potatoes Au Gratin	11-1/2 oz.	Remove from foil container. Place in 2-qt. container. Stir twice.	7-9 min., covered.
Scalloped Potatoes	12 oz.	Remove from foil container. Place in 2-qt. container. Stir twice.	7-8 min., covered.

NAME	AMOUNT	DIRECTIONS	TIME
Tater Tots Potatoes	16 oz.	Place on a paper towel.	9-11 min., uncovered.
Spinach Soufflé	12 oz.	Remove from foil. Place in 2-qt. container. Don't stir. Rotate 1/4 turn every 2 min.	7-9 min., covered.
Buttered Zucchini or Eggplant Sticks	16 oz.	Arrange in a spoke pattern on a paper towel.	2 min. 30 sec., uncovered.

Butter Melting and Softening Guide

Melting	3 tablespoons	15 sec.
	1/4 cup	30 sec.
	1/2 cup	37 sec.
	1 cup	45 sec.
Softening	1/2 cup	5 sec. Stand 5 sec. Cook 5 sec.
	1 cup	10 sec. Stand 5 sec. Cook 10 sec.

Asparagus Pie

1 **prepared pie shell**
1 **egg white,** slightly beaten
2 (10-ounce) packages frozen **asparagus,** thawed, drained
1-1/4 cups **béchamel sauce** (See page 50.)
2-1/2 cups **Swiss cheese,** grated

1. Use a pastry brush to coat pie shell with egg white. Prick with fork tines. Cook 3 minutes, uncovered.

2. Place asparagus in the pie shell and pour sauce over it. Sprinkle with cheese.

3. Cook 2 minutes, uncovered; rest 1 minute. Repeat until pie has cooked 9-10 minutes. Rotate pie plate 1/4 turn every 2 minutes.

4. Brown in the microwave oven with browning element or conventionally.

5. Cool on wire rack. Serve warm.

Makes 6-8 servings.

Amish Beans

5 slices **bacon**
1/2 cup **sugar**
1/2 cup **vinegar**
3 tablespoons instant **minced onion**
2 (10-ounce) packages frozen **green beans**, thawed

1. In a rectangular container, cook bacon 3 minutes, loosely covered with a paper towel. Stir every 30 seconds. Remove bacon with slotted spoon; crumble.

2. In a 1-quart container, place bacon and 3 tablespoons grease. Add sugar, vinegar, and onion; stir. Cook 30 seconds, uncovered. (Sugar must be dissolved.)

3. Add green beans; cook 13 minutes, covered. Let stand 3 minutes, covered.

Makes 6-8 servings.

Bar-B-Q Baked Beans

3 slices **bacon**, cut in 5 sections
5 tablespoons instant **minced onion** or 1 medium **onion**, chopped
2 tablespoons dried **sweet pepper flakes** or 1/2 cup **pepper**, diced
2 (16-ounce) cans **baked beans**, partially drained
1-1/2 cups **barbecue sauce** (see page 43) or **catsup**

1. In a rectangular 2-quart container, cook bacon 3 minutes, loosely covered with a paper towel. Stir every 30 seconds. Pour off all but 2 tablespoons grease.

2. Add onions and sweet pepper. (Fresh onion and pepper cook 2 minutes, uncovered; dried onion and pepper cook 1 minute, uncovered.)

3. Add beans and liquid.

4. Add barbecue sauce and bacon; stir. Cook 10 minutes, covered.

Makes 6-8 servings.

Green Bean Casserole

1 (8-ounce) can **bean sprouts** or 1-1/2 cups fresh **bean sprouts**
2 (10-ounce) packages frozen **green beans**, cooked
1 (10 1/2-ounce) can **cream of chicken soup**
1 (10 1/2-ounce) can **cream of mushroom soup**
1 (3-ounce) can **french fried onions**
1/2 cup canned **grated Parmesan cheese**

1. In a 2-quart container, combine bean sprouts, green beans, and soups.

2. Add 1/2 can onions to mixture; stir.

3. Top with remaining 1/2 can onions. Cook 12-14 minutes, uncovered.

4. Sprinkle with cheese. Brown in microwave oven with browning element or conventionally.

Makes 6-8 servings.

NOTE: For best results, use fresh bean sprouts.

Indian Bean Bake

2 (15-ounce) cans **navy beans** with liquid
4 teaspoons instant **minced onion** or 1 medium **onion** (1 cup), minced
1/3 to 1/2 cup **chutney**, finely minced
1 teaspoon **dry mustard**
Salt and **pepper** to taste
1/3 to 1/2 cup **yogurt** (optional)

1. In a 1 1/2-quart container, combine all ingredients except the yogurt.
2. Cook 8 minutes, covered.
3. Add yogurt just before serving.

Makes 6-8 servings.

Italian Garbanzo Beans

2 (15-ounce) cans **garbanzo beans**, drained
1 (14 1/2-ounce) can **stewed tomatoes**
3 tablespoons dried **sweet pepper flakes**
1/2 (1 1/2-ounce) envelope **Italian spaghetti sauce**
1 tablespoon instant **minced onion**
Salt and **pepper** to taste

1. In a 2-quart container, combine all ingredients; stir.

2. Cook 10-11 minutes, covered.

Makes 6-8 servings.

Barbecued Limas

3 slices **bacon**, cut in 5 sections
3 tablespoons instant **minced onion**
1 (10-ounce) package frozen **lima beans**, thawed
1/2 teaspoon **garlic salt**
1 (10 1/2-ounce) can **tomato soup**
1 teaspoon **Worcestershire sauce**
1 teaspoon **vinegar**
1 teaspoon **prepared mustard**
1 teaspoon **chili powder**
Salt and **pepper** to taste

1. In a rectangular 1 1/2-quart container, cook bacon 3 minutes, loosely covered with a paper towel. Stir every 30 seconds. Pour off all but 2 tablespoons grease.

2. Cook onion in bacon grease 1 minute, uncovered. Add remaining ingredients; stir.

3. Cook 10 minutes, covered.

Makes 4-6 servings.

NOTE: This recipe is better prepared the day before serving to allow flavors to mingle.

Oriental Bean Sprout Casserole

2 (10-ounce) packages frozen **pea pods** or 2 (10 1/2-ounce) packages frozen french-cut **green beans**, thawed
1 (6-ounce) can **water chestnuts**, drained, cut in pieces
1/2 cup **milk**
2 (2-ounce) cans **mushrooms**
Soy sauce to taste
1 (15-ounce) can **bean sprouts** or 1-1/2 cups fresh **bean sprouts**

1. In a 1 1/2-quart container, combine all ingredients except bean sprouts. Cook 10 minutes, covered.

2. Add bean sprouts and stir. Let stand 2 minutes, covered.

Makes 6-8 servings.

NOTE: For best results, use fresh bean sprouts.

Beets with Orange Sauce

1 (16-ounce) can **beets,** drained
3/4 cup **orange marmalade**
2 teaspoons **cinnamon**
1/4 teaspoon **cloves**
1/2 teaspoon **allspice**
1/2 cup **orange juice**
4 teaspoons **butter**
1/8 teaspoon **salt**

1. In a 1-quart container, combine all ingredients.

2. Cook 6-8 minutes, covered. Stir twice.

Makes 4-6 servings.

Broccoli and Cheese

1 (6-ounce) package **cream cheese**
1/4 cup **water**
1/2 cup **milk**
1 (10-ounce) package frozen **broccoli,** thawed
4 **eggs,** hard cooked, chopped
1 (2-ounce) can **pimentos**
1/3 cup **cracker crumbs**
1/3 cup **sherry**

1. In a 2-quart container, soften cream cheese. Cook 1 minute.

2. Add water and milk. Stir until cheese is blended into liquid.

3. Add broccoli, eggs, and pimentos. Cook 10 minutes, covered.

4. Remove from oven. Sprinkle with cracker crumbs and pour sherry over the top.

5. Brown in the microwave oven with browning element or conventionally.

Makes 4-6 servings.

Red Cabbage and Wine

2 (16-ounce) cans **red cabbage**
4 **apples,** peeled, cored, sliced
5 tablespoons instant **minced onion** or 1 cup **onions,** chopped
2 teaspoons **garlic salt**
1/4 teaspoon **carraway seed**
1/4 teaspoon **nutmeg**
1/4 teaspoon **allspice**
1/4 teaspoon **cinnamon**
1/8 teaspoon **thyme**
2 teaspoons dried **orange peel**
1/4 cup **butter,** melted
Salt and **pepper** to taste
1 **bay leaf**
3 tablespoons **brown sugar**
2 tablespoons **wine vinegar**
3 tablespoons **red currant** jelly
1-1/2 cups **red wine**

1. In a 2-quart container, layer cabbage, apples, and onions.

2. Sprinkle spices and pour butter over each layer. Salt and pepper to taste. Place bay leaf on top.

3. Sprinkle with brown sugar and pour vinegar over the top. Dot with jelly. Pour wine over all.

4. Cook 10-12 minutes, covered. Rotate 1/4 turn every 3 minutes.

Makes 6-8 servings.

Creamy Chard

2 (10-ounce) packages frozen **Swiss chard,** thawed
2 tablespoons **butter**
1 (8-ounce) package **cream cheese,** cubed
Salt and **pepper**
1/4 cup **white wine**

1. In a 1-quart container, combine chard and butter. Cook 7 minutes, covered. Stir twice.
2. Add cubed cream cheese. Salt and pepper to taste.
3. Pour wine over the top.
4. Cook 5-6 minutes, covered. Stir once.

Makes 6-8 servings.

Cauliflower and Squash Casserole

1 (10-ounce) package frozen **zucchini**, thawed
1/2 (10-ounce) package frozen **cauliflower**, thawed
2 tablespoons **butter**
1/3 cup **milk**
1 (4-ounce) can **mushrooms**, with liquid
1-1/2 tablespoons instant **minced onion**
1/4 cup **bread crumbs**
1 cup **cheddar cheese**, shredded
1/4 teaspoon **chili powder**
Salt and **pepper** to taste

1. In a 1 1/2-quart container, combine zucchini, cauliflower, and butter. Cook 10 minutes, uncovered.
2. Mash zucchini and cauliflower. Add the remaining ingredients; stir.
3. Cook 5-6 minutes, covered.

Makes 4-6 servings.

Mexican Corn Bake

4 **eggs**, beaten
4 (17-ounce) cans **cream-style corn**
1-1/2 cups **corn meal**
1 (2-ounce) jar **pimentos**
1-1/2 teaspoons **garlic powder**
1 teaspoon **baking powder**
3/4 cup **vegetable oil**
1 (2-ounce) can **mushrooms**
1 (4-ounce) can **green chilies**, chopped
Salt and **pepper** to taste
1 pound **cheddar cheese**, grated

1. In a 3-quart container, combine all ingredients except cheese.
2. Cook 10-12 minutes, covered.
3. Sprinkle with cheese.
4. Brown in the microwave oven with browning element or conventionally.

Makes 6-8 servings.

Eggplant

4 small **eggplants**
6 tablespoons dried **sweet pepper flakes**
5 tablespoons **vegetable oil**
6 tablespoons instant **minced onion**
2 tablespoons dried **parsley flakes**
4 medium **tomatoes**, diced
1 cup canned **grated Parmesan cheese**

1. Pierce eggplants and cook 2 at a time on wax paper 13-15 minutes, uncovered.
2. Cut each eggplant in half, lengthwise. Take out meat and place in a 2-quart container. (Save shells.)
3. Add remaining ingredients except Parmesan cheese. Cook 4 minutes, covered. Stir once.
4. Prepare topping.
5. Refill eggplant shells. Pour topping over each; sprinkle with Parmesan cheese. Cook 1 minute, uncovered.

Topping

1 cup **nuts**, ground
3/4 cup **wheat germ**
2 tablespoons **butter**, melted

In a small bowl, combine nuts, wheat germ, and butter.

Makes 4-8 servings.

Eggplant Casserole

1 large **eggplant**
2 tablespoons dried **sweet pepper flakes**
3 tablespoons instant **minced onion**
1/2 (6-ounce) package **stuffing**
1 (10 1/2-ounce) can **cream of mushroom soup**
1/3 cup **milk**
2 **eggs**, beaten

1. Prick eggplant; cook 10 minutes, uncovered, on wax paper.

2. Peel and cut in sections.

3. In a 2-quart container, place the eggplant, sweet pepper, onion, and stuffing; mix.

4. In a bowl, combine soup, milk, and eggs; stir until smooth. Pour over the eggplant mixture.

5. Cook 5-7 minutes, covered. Stir twice.

Makes 4 servings.

Dry Herbs

4 or 5 fresh **herb branches**
Paper towels
Jars and lids

1. Wash herbs and shake off excess water.

2. Place herbs between 2 paper towels.

3. Cook 2-3 minutes.

4. If not brittle and dry, recook for 30 seconds.

5. Separate leaves and/or flowers from the stalks and place between 2 sheets of wax paper. Crush with a rolling pin.

6. Store in sealed jars.

7. Add dried herbs directly to food; no soaking is necessary.

NOTE: Dry herb seeds the same way; when dried, rub to remove chaff. SEE MANUFACTURER'S INSTRUCTIONS FOR DRYING.

Scalloped Onions

1 (1-pound 4-ounce) package frozen small **onions**, thawed
2 tablespoons **butter**, melted
1 (10 1/2-ounce) can **white sauce**
1/4 teaspoon **paprika**
Salt and **pepper** to taste
1/4 cup **white wine**
2 cups **cheddar cheese**, grated

1. In a 1 1/2-quart container, combine all ingredients except cheese.

2. Cook 8-10 minutes, covered. Stir twice.

3. Add cheese; stir. Cook 1 minute, uncovered.

4. Brown in the microwave oven with browning element or conventionally.

Makes 6-8 servings.

Mexican Peas

1/2 cup **onions**, chopped
3 teaspoons **butter**, melted
1 (10-ounce) package frozen **peas**, thawed
1 cup **cottage cheese**

1. In a 1-quart container, cook onions in butter 2 minutes, uncovered.

2. Add peas. Cook 5 minutes.

3. Add cottage cheese. Cook 2 minutes; stir every 30 seconds.

Makes 4-6 servings.

Mexican Potatoes

1-1/4 cup **milk**
1 (1 1/2-ounce) envelope **chili seasoning mix**
2 (15-ounce) cans small, whole **potatoes**, drained
Salt and **pepper** to taste

1. In a 3-quart container, combine milk and chili seasoning mix; stir. Cook 1 minute, uncovered.

2. Add potatoes, salt, and pepper. Cook 6-7 minutes, covered. Stir once.

Makes 6-8 servings.

Scalloped Potatoes

6 cups **potatoes**, sliced, or
3 (10-ounce) packages frozen **chopped potatoes**, thawed
1-1/2 cups **milk**
1/2 cup instant **minced onion**
2 cups **American cheese**, cubed
1 (2-ounce) can **pimentos**, diced
3 tablespoons dried **parsley flakes**
Salt and **pepper** to taste

1. In a 2 1/2-quart container, combine all ingredients.

2. Cook 13-15 minutes, covered. Stir every 5 minutes.

3. Cook 3 minutes, uncovered.

4. Brown in the microwave oven with browning element or conventionally.

Makes 6-8 servings.

Southern Sweet Potatoes

1 cup **butter**
1 cup **sugar**
1 (16-ounce) can **sweet potatoes**, mashed
1/2 cup **milk**
1 teaspoon powdered **ginger**
3 teaspoons dried **orange peel**

1. In a 1-quart container, cream butter and sugar until light and fluffy.

2. Add the remaining ingredients. Stir until smooth.

3. Cook 6 minutes, covered. Stir once.

Makes 4-6 servings.

Swiss Spinach

2 (10-ounce) packages frozen chopped spinach, thawed
3 eggs, beaten
2 cups cottage cheese
Salt and pepper to taste
3/4 cup canned grated Parmesan cheese

1. In a 1 1/2-quart container, combine ingredients except 1/4 cup Parmesan cheese.

2. Cook 9-10 minutes, covered. Stir twice.

3. Sprinkle Parmesan cheese over the top. Cook 2 minutes, uncovered.

Makes 6-8 servings.

Zucchini Roma

6-8 medium, fresh zucchini
Salt and pepper to taste
1 cup sour cream
1 cup cheddar cheese, shredded

1. Cut each zucchini in half; cook on wax paper 7-9 minutes, uncovered, in spoke pattern.

2. Place in a flat container and add salt and pepper.

3. Cover each zucchini half with sour cream, and sprinkle with cheese. Cook 2 minutes, uncovered.

Makes 6-8 servings.

BREADS

A German folk saying, "Whose bread I eat, her song I sing," shows the importance man has always placed on the staff of life. At one time, bakers could be publicly whipped or have their ears nailed to a post for baking inferior bread. A lesser punishment entailed standing in the pillory with the offending bread tied around the neck. If only they had had the fail-safe bread mixes we enjoy today.

Prepared mixes are the secret in most of the bread recipes. The microwaves do not brown, so you may wish to add yellow food coloring to the batter when not using a dark grain flour base. The batter rises higher when cooked in the microwave oven, so fill your containers only half full. Make one or two muffins out of any leftover batter.

Breads: Points to Remember

1. All breads cook well in the microwave oven.
2. Cook breads uncovered.
3. The batter rises higher than that of conventionally cooked bread; therefore, fill containers only half full.
4. Microwaves do not brown; therefore, add yellow food coloring to white bread or use a glaze. Dark breads or those using brown sugar look best.

5. When using batters that you prepare, use only half leavening ingredient, such as yeast or baking powder.
6. Any extra batter can be cooked in cupcake paper liners placed in custard cups. See guide (page 198). If liners are unavailable, use greased custard cups.
7. Toothpick test all muffins and casserole-type breads. Bread is done when toothpick inserted in center comes out clean.
8. Coffee cakes cook best in ten x six-inch container.
9. Make garlic butter and heat it before spreading on bread; this process enhances the flavor.
10. To speed up cooking time when cooking bread conventionally, first cook in the microwave oven three minutes; then cook conventionally at 450 degrees in a preheated oven about eight minutes or until done.
11. Reheat bread on a paper towel, napkin, paper plate, or in a straw basket tucked inside a cloth or paper napkin. As the bread heats, the moisture comes to the outside; using paper products or a cloth napkin allows this moisture to escape.
12. Use the microwave oven to thaw and proof frozen yeast bread dough. Lightly butter a one-pound, frozen, uncooked bread loaf. Place in a greased loaf pan. To thaw and proof, cook 15 seconds and stand three minutes. Repeat until bread has cooked three minutes or doubles in size. Touch dough after first two minutes to make sure it is not too hot. Cook, uncovered, five minutes or until there are no doughy spots.
13. Nut breads tend to cook unevenly. Cook first two minutes the microwave method, and then cook conventionally about eight minutes at 450 degrees in a preheated oven.
14. Prepare bread crumbs and cubes by placing on wax paper and cooking two to three minutes. Stir five times.

Bread Convenience Foods Guide

Boxed

NAME	AMOUNT	DIRECTIONS	COOK
Cornbread Mix	16 oz.	Prepare according to pkg. directions. Pour batter into greased 1 1/2-qt. (9 x 5-inch) loaf pan. Rotate 1/3 turn every 2 min.	6 min.
Fruit and Nut Bread Mix	15-1/2 to 17 oz.	Prepare according to pkg. directions. Pour into 1 1/2-qt. (9 x 5-inch) wax-paper-lined loaf pan. Rotate 1/4 turn every 2 min.	7-8 min. Stand 10 min.
Hot Yeast Roll Mix	13-1/2 oz.	Prepare according to pkg. directions. (Add yellow food coloring—optional.) Put dough in a greased 1 1/2-qt. (9 x 5-inch) loaf pan. Let rise.	5-6 min. or until no doughy spots.
Muffin Mix	13 oz.	Prepare according to pkg. directions. Fill cupcake paper liners 1/2 full. Place in custard cups or shallow cups. Place in a circular pattern. Cook 6 at a time.	2 min. 30 sec. to 3 min.

Fresh

Directions: Place precooked bread item on paper towel, paper plate, or cloth napkin. Cook, uncovered. For several slices of bread, use a straw basket covered with a napkin. If overcooked, the bread items turn tough or rubbery because there is more moisture on the inside than in the crust.

NAME	AMOUNT	TIME (AT ROOM TEMPERATURE)	TIME (FROZEN)	ADDITIONAL TIME
Bagels	1	10-12 sec.	20-22 sec.	Add 5 sec. for each additional bagel.
Bread Slices	1	5 sec.	15 sec.	Add 10 sec. for each additional slice.
Coffee Cakes	11 oz.	45 sec. Stand 25 sec. Cook 1 min. Stand 30 sec.	1 min. 30 sec. Stand 25 sec. Cook 1 min.	

NAME	AMOUNT	TIME (AT ROOM TEMPERATURE)	TIME (FROZEN)	ADDITIONAL TIME
Coffee Cakes	1 piece	7-10 sec.	20 sec.	Add 5 sec. for each additional piece.
Dinner Rolls	1	8-10 sec.	20 sec.	Add 5 sec. for each additional roll.
Doughnuts	1	10 sec.	25 sec.	Add 10 sec. for each additional doughnut.
French Toasts	1	30 sec.	1 min.	Add 15 sec. for each additional piece (60 sec. if frozen).
Pancakes	1	20 sec.	45 sec.	Add 25-30 sec. for each additional pancake.
Sweet Rolls	1	15 sec.	20 sec.	Add 5 sec. for each additional sweet roll.
Toaster Pastries	1	10-15 sec.	25 sec.	Add 5 sec. for each additional pastry. Use maximum time for refrigerated types and for Danish.
Waffles	1 section	15 sec.	20 sec.	Add 10-15 sec. for each additional waffle.

Christmas Biscuits

3 cups **dry biscuit mix**
3/4 cup **sugar**
1/2 teaspoon **ground coriander**
1/4 teaspoon **cinnamon**
1 **egg**, beaten
1-1/4 cups **milk**
1-1/2 cups **pecans**, chopped
1 cup dried, glazed, **mixed fruit**, chopped
20-24 cupcake paper liners

1. In a bowl, combine biscuit mix, sugar, coriander, cinnamon, egg, and milk. Beat until smooth.

2. Stir in nuts and glazed fruits.

3. Fill each cupcake paper liner 1/2 full. Place in custard cups. Cook 6 at a time in a circular pattern. Cook 3 minutes, uncovered.

Makes 14-16 biscuits.

Cinnamon-Pecan Biscuits

2 tablespoons **butter**
1/3 cup **brown sugar**
1 teaspoon **cinnamon**
1/2 cup **pecans**, chopped
1 (8-ounce) package refrigerated **biscuits**

1. Cook butter in a glass pie plate 15 seconds, uncovered. Spread evenly over pie plate.

2. Sprinkle brown sugar, cinnamon, and pecans over the bottom of the pie plate. Leave center empty.

3. Place biscuits on top of mixture. Arrange in a ring around the edge. Press into mixture.

4. Cook 3 minutes, loosely covered with paper towel. Let stand 15 seconds. Invert pie plate over wax paper. Let stand 3 or 4 minutes before serving.

Makes 8 biscuits.

Yogurt-Onion Biscuit Bread

2 cups **dry biscuit mix**
1/2 cup plus 1 tablespoon **cold water**
1/2 cup instant **minced onion**
3 **eggs**, beaten
1 (1-ounce) container plain **yogurt**
1/8 teaspoon **salt**

1. In a bowl, combine biscuit mix, water, and onion.

2. On a floured board, roll dough into an 11-inch square.

3. Place in a 10 x 10 x 2-inch greased container. Pat up the sides.

4. In a bowl, combine egg, yogurt, and salt. Pour over biscuit mix.

5. Cook 7 minutes 30 seconds to 8 minutes, uncovered. Rotate 1/3 turn every 2 minutes. Tip container back and forth to spread yogurt mixture evenly over the dough.

6. Brown in the microwave oven with browning element or conventionally.

7. Cool on wire rack 5-10 minutes.

Makes about 8-10 servings.

Health-Food Nut Biscuits

2 cups **dry biscuit mix**
1 **egg**, beaten
3/4 cup **milk**
1/4 cup **vegetable oil**
2 tablespoons **honey**
1-1/3 cups **whole bran cereal**
4 tablespoons **wheat germ**
3 tablespoons **sugar**
1/2 cup **pecans** or **walnuts**
12-14 cupcake paper liners

1. In a bowl, combine all ingredients. Batter will be slightly lumpy.

2. Fill each cupcake paper liner 1/2 full. Place in custard cups. Cook 6 at a time in a circular pattern 2 minutes 30 seconds to 3 minutes, uncovered.

Makes 12-14 biscuits.

Carrot Corn Bread

5 pieces **bacon**, cooked, crumbled
1 (13-ounce) box **corn bread mix**
1 cup **water**
2 **eggs**, beaten
1 cup **carrots**, shredded
2 tablespoons instant **minced onion**

1. Cook bacon. See guide (page 92).

2. Combine corn bread mix, water, and eggs.

3. Add carrots, minced onion, and crumbled bacon pieces; stir.

4. Pour into a 2-quart greased container. Cook 6 minutes 30 seconds to 7 minutes, uncovered. Rotate 1/3 turn every 2 minutes.

5. Cool on wire rack 5-10 minutes.

Corn and Cheese Bread

1 (15-ounce) box **corn muffin mix**
1 egg, beaten
2 tablespoons **cream**
1/2 teaspoon **garlic salt**
1 tablespoon dried **parsley flakes**
3 tablespoons instant **minced onion**
1 cup **cheddar cheese soup**
3 tablespoons **butter**
2 tablespoons canned **grated Parmesan cheese**
3 tablespoons fine **bread crumbs**

1. In a bowl, combine corn muffin mix, eggs, cream, garlic, parsley, onion, and soup.

2. Pour batter into an 8-inch square greased container.

3. In a small container, cook butter and Parmesan cheese 30 seconds, uncovered.

4. Pour butter over the corn muffin mixture. Sprinkle bread crumbs over the top.

5. Cook 9-10 minutes, uncovered. Rotate bread 1/4 turn every 2 minutes.

6. Cool on wire rack 5-10 minutes.

Mexican Spoon Bread

1 (13-ounce) box **corn muffin mix**
1/2 (16-ounce) can **cream-style corn**
2 tablespoons **vegetable oil**
2 **eggs**, beaten
3 tablespoons instant **minced onion**
1 (4-ounce) can **jalapeno chili peppers**, chopped
1 cup **cheddar cheese**, grated

1. In a bowl, combine all ingredients except chili peppers and cheese.

2. Pour 1/2 batter into greased 2-quart container.

3. Spread chilies and sprinkle 1/2 of the cheese over the top. Pour remaining batter over chilies and cheese. Sprinkle remaining cheese over the top.

4. Cook 6-7 minutes, uncovered. Rotate bread 1/4 turn every 2 minutes.

5. Cool on wire rack 5-10 minutes.

Onion-Cheese Casserole Bread

2 cups **dry biscuit mix**
1/2 cup cold **water**
10 **green onions and tops**, diced
1/2 cup **ham**, cooked, chopped
1 teaspoon **garlic salt**
1/2 cup canned grated **Parmesan cheese**
1 teaspoon **dry mustard**
1 tablespoon **butter**

1. In a bowl, combine all ingredients except butter.

2. Cook butter in a 2-quart container 30 seconds, uncovered. Spread evenly over container.

3. Place batter in container and cook 6-7 minutes, uncovered. Rotate 1/4 turn every 2 minutes.

4. Invert on plate and cook 1 minute, uncovered.

6. Cool on wire rack for 5-10 minutes.

Rye-Graham Bread

3/4 (1/4-ounce) package **dry yeast**
3 cups **water**, lukewarm
1 cup instant **mashed potato flakes**
1 tablespoon **sugar**
2 teaspoons **salt**
1 cup **rye-graham flour**
4 cups **white flour**
2 tablespoons **butter**, melted

1. In a bowl, dissolve yeast in warm water.

2. Mix in potato flakes, sugar, and salt.

3. Add rye-graham and white flour, 1/2 cup at a time. Stir after first 3 cups, then knead dough after each addition of flour.

4. Let rise in a warm place.

5. Place dough in lightiy greased loaf pan. Use a pastry brush to coat the top with butter. Let rise again.

6. Cook 5-6 minutes, uncovered.

White Yeast Bread

1/4 cup **sugar**
2 tablespoons **shortening**
1 teaspoon **salt**
1 cup **hot water**
1 **egg**, beaten
3/4 **yeast cake,** dissolved in
 1/4 cup warm **water**
3-1/2 to 4 cups **flour**, sifted
2 tablespoons **butter**, melted

1. In a bowl, combine all ingredients except flour and butter.

2. Add flour 1/2 cup at a time. Stir after first 3 cups, then knead dough after each addition of flour. (Dough should be stiff.)

3. Let rise in a warm place. Place dough in lightly greased glass loaf pan.

4. Use a pastry brush to coat the top of the dough with butter. Let rise again.

5. Cook 5-6 minutes. Brown in microwave with browning element or conventionally.

NOTE: Recipe also makes 12 rolls.

Zucchini Bread

2 cups **dry biscuit mix**
2 **eggs**, beaten
1 cup **sugar**
3/4 cup **vegetable oil**
2 cups **zucchini**, grated
3 teaspoons **vanilla** extract
1 teaspoon **salt**
1 teaspoon **cinnamon**

1. In a bowl, combine biscuit mix, eggs, sugar, oil, and zucchini.

2. Add vanilla, salt, and cinnamon; stir.

3. Pour batter into an 8-inch square greased container. Cook 10 minutes to 11 minutes 30 seconds, uncovered. Rotate 1/4 turn every 2 minutes.

4. Cool on wire rack 5-10 minutes.

Doughnut Turns

2 cups **dry biscuit mix**
1/3 cup **cream**
2 **eggs**
2-1/2 tablespoons **sugar**
1 teaspoon **nutmeg**
1 teaspoon **cinnamon**

1. In a bowl, combine all ingredients.

2. On floured board, roll out dough into a 1/2-inch thick rectangle. Cut with floured doughnut cutter.

3. Twist each doughnut to make a figure 8. Place doughnut holes and figure 8s on an ungreased, flat container.

4. Cook 3 minutes 30 seconds to 4 minutes, uncovered. Rotate 1/2 turn every 2 minutes.

5. While hot, coat with sugar icing.

Icing

1/2 cup **butter**, melted
1/2 cup **sugar**

In a bowl, combine ingredients.

Makes 14-16 doughnuts.

Banana Gingerbread

2 tablespoons **lemon juice**
2 cups **bananas**, mashed
1 (14-ounce) package **gingerbread mix**
2 tablespoons **vegetable oil**
1 cup **raisins**
1/2 cup **pecans**

1. Pour lemon on bananas and mash.
2. In a bowl, add bananas, oil, raisins, and nuts to the gingerbread mix. Stir until smooth.
3. Pour batter into greased cake pan or glass or plastic gingerbread mold.
4. Cook 6-7 minutes, uncovered. Rotate 1/4 turn every 2 minutes.
5. Cool on wire rack 5-10 minutes.

Applesauce, Pumpkin, or Banana Muffins

2 cups **dry biscuit mix**
1/3 cup **sugar**
1 teaspoon **cinnamon**
1/8 teaspoon **nutmeg**
3/4 cup **canned applesauce** or **pumpkin**, or **fresh banana**, mashed
1/4 cup **buttermilk**
1 **egg**, beaten
1 tablespoon **vegetable oil**
14-16 cupcake paper liners

1. In a bowl, combine dry ingredients.
2. In another bowl, combine fruit, buttermilk, egg, and oil.
3. Add the fruit mixture to the dry ingredients; stir until smooth.
4. Fill each cupcake paper liner 1/2 full. Place in custard cups. Cook 6 at a time in a circular pattern. Cook 2 minutes 30 seconds, uncovered.

Makes 14-16 muffins.

NOTE: Canned baby food may be substituted for the applesauce and banana.

Granola Muffins

3 cups **dry biscuit mix**
3/4 cup **milk**
1/4 cup **vegetable oil**
1 **egg**, beaten
3 tablespoons **honey**
2 cups **granola**
1/2 cup **raisins**
1/2 cup **nuts**
18 cupcake paper liners

1. In a bowl, combine biscuit mix, milk, oil, egg, and honey. Batter will be slightly lumpy.

2. Add granola, raisins, and nuts; stir.

3. Fill each cupcake paper liner 1/2 full. Place in custard cups. Cook 6 at a time in a circular pattern. Cook 2 minutes, uncovered.

Makes 16-18 muffins.

Orange-Rum Muffins

1 (14-ounce) package **orange muffin mix**
1 (8-ounce) can **crushed pineapple**, drained
2/3 cup **rum** or **orange liqueur**
1/4 teaspoon dried **orange peel**
1 **egg**, beaten
1/3 cup **pecans**, chopped
12 cupcake paper liners

1. In a bowl, combine all ingredients; stir to moisten.

2. Fill each cupcake paper liner 1/2 full. Place in custard cups. Cook 6 at a time in a circular pattern. Cook 3 minutes, uncovered.

Makes 10-12 muffins.

Fast Cinnamon Rolls

1 (1/4-ounce) package **active dry yeast**
1/2 cup **warm water**
1 **egg**, beaten
2 tablespoons **white sugar**
3 cups **dry biscuit mix**
3 tablespoons **butter,** melted
1 tablespoon **cinnamon**
1 tablespoon **brown sugar**
1 cup **pecans**, chopped
1/2 cup **butter**
6 tablespoons **butter**

1. In a bowl, dissolve yeast in warm water. Add egg, white sugar, and biscuit mix. Beat until smooth.

2. Knead dough on floured board about 50 times.

3. Separate dough into two parts. Roll one into a 12 x 5-inch rectangle.

4. Pour butter and sprinkle cinnamon, brown sugar, and nuts over the dough. Roll up jelly-roll fashion. Seal by pinching edge of dough into the roll.

5. Cook 1/2 cup butter in a glass pie plate 1 minute, uncovered. Spread evenly over pie plate.

6. Cut 1-inch slices and place cut part up in buttered pie plate. Let rise 1 hour in a warm, dry place.

7. Cook 5-6 minutes, uncovered. Let stand 15 seconds. Invert pie plate over wax paper. Let stand 3 or 4 minutes before serving.

Makes 18-20 rolls.

NOTE: For even faster cinnamon rolls, replace biscuit dough with defrosted, frozen bread. Fill and cook.

Date-Nut Rolls

1 (8-ounce) package refrigerated **crescent rolls**
4 tablespoons **butter**, melted
1/2 cup **brown sugar**
1-1/2 teaspoons **sugar**
1 teaspoon **cinnamon**
1/2 cup **pecans** or **walnuts,** chopped
1 (8- or 10-ounce) package **pitted dates,** chopped

1. Separate the crescent rolls into triangles and lay flat on a floured breadboard.
2. Cook butter 30 seconds, uncovered.
3. On each triangular roll, pour butter, sprinkle sugar and cinnamon, and place nuts and dates.
4. Roll up and pinch closed. Place each roll, seam side down, on a pyrex pizza plate or other flat container.
5. Cook 3-4 minutes, uncovered. Rotate 1/4 turn every 2 minutes.

Makes 8 rolls.

DESSERTS

"Tis the Dessert that graces all the Feast—for an ill end disparages the rest," said Dr. William King. For many people, the last course of a meal is often enjoyed the most, but desserts do not have to accompany meals only. You can eat desserts almost any time of the day or night. They are also the main attraction for many festivities. At one time, honey and fruit syrup were the only sweeteners used in most parts of the world. Without sugar many of our desserts could not have been created. You will find cakes, pies, cookies, custards, fruits, puddings, and other tasty sweets listed in this section.

Sugar, first known as "Indian salt," probably came from the Sanskrit *sarkara*. After the refining of sugar, in 1420, its use increased. Even though refinery techniques were perfected by 1471, sugar continued to be quite expensive, and only druggists (or apothecaries as they were called) handled it. Considered a great medicine, it sold by the ounce. Despite the high price, cooks still purchased it; however, by about the sixteenth century, the price came down and sugar became popular in foods we now term desserts.

Microwave ovens cut dessert cooking time in half, and this can come in handy. When we first moved into our house, I didn't know anyone. Despite this, I gave a birthday party for one of my boys. Unknown to me, my son Blake invited all the mothers. I asked them to join me in the kitchen. While we got acquainted, I quickly made the orange cake on page 204. They soon realized they hadn't really been invited, but we were having so much fun it didn't seem to matter. Lasting friendships were made at that mother-and-son birthday party.

Dessert Convenience Foods Guide

Frozen

NAME	AMOUNT	DIRECTIONS	TIME
Apple and Cherry Blintzes	15 oz. (6)	Place on paper towel. Turn after 5 min. Arrange in a circular pattern.	10 min., uncovered.
Apple Dumplings	12-1/2 oz. (4)	Place on paper towel. Turn after 5 min.	8 min., uncovered.
Apple Fritters	12 oz.	Place on paper towel.	9-10 min., uncovered.
Cinnamon Streusel	10-7/8 oz.	Remove cover.	8-10 min.
Corn Fritters	12 oz.	Place on paper towel.	9-10 min., uncovered.
Fruit Turnovers	12-1/2 oz. (4)	Place on paper towel.	10-12 min., uncovered.
Peach Cobbler	32 oz.	Remove from foil container. Place in 2-qt. container. Rotate 1/4 turn every 3 min.	25 min., uncovered.

Cakes: Points to Remember

1. Let cake stand ten minutes in cake pan before cooking for a more even crust.
2. Grease only the bottom of the cake pan.
3. Because cakes rise higher in the microwave oven, fill containers only half full.
4. Make cupcakes out of any extra batter.
5. When using your own recipe, reduce leavening, such as baking powder, by one-quarter.
6. To reduce the problem of a doughy center, elevate the cake by setting the filled glass cake pan on an inverted saucer or second inverted glass cake pan.

7. Rotate cakes several times during cooking period.
8. Cakes do not brown on top.
9. The cake is done when a toothpick inserted in the center comes out clean.
10. When the cake is done, moist areas may be on the cake surface. Additional cooking time does not help and may overcook other areas.
11. Layer cakes are easier to frost when refrigerated a few hours.
12. To speed up cooking time when cooking conventionally, bake 15 minutes in a preheated oven at 375 degrees, then cook the microwave method from two to four minutes, uncovered.

Cake Guide

Cakes

Fill cake pans half full.

8- to 9-inch round glass pan	About 5-6 min.
8 x 8-inch glass pan	About 7-8 min.
12 x 8 x 2-inch glass pan	About 9-10 min.
9 x 5 x 3-inch glass loaf pan	About 7-8 min.

Cupcakes

Cook in cupcake paper liners placed inside custard cups or shallow coffee cups. Position in a circular pattern in the oven.

1 cupcake	About 25-30 sec.
2 cupcakes	About 1 min.
3 cupcakes	About 1 min. 15 sec.
4 cupcakes	About 1 min. 30 sec. to 2 min.
5 cupcakes	About 2 min. 30 sec.
6 cupcakes	About 3 min.

Bundt Cake

9-cup glass bundt pan (or layer)	About 9-12 min.
cupcakes	Add 25-30 sec. to the above cupcake time.

NOTE: Makc cupcakes from any extra batter. For refrigerated batter, increase cooking time 5 minutes.

Cake Convenience Foods Guide

Room Temperature

NAME	AMOUNT	DIRECTIONS	TIME
Rewarm cake	1 serving	Place on napkin.	15 sec., uncovered.

Frozen

NAME	AMOUNT	DIRECTIONS	TIME
Cake, Unfrosted	1 serving	Place on napkin.	15 sec., uncovered.
	about 17 oz.	Place on paper plate or leave on styrofoam tray.	10 sec. Stand 15 sec. Cook 5 sec. Stand 1 min. Lightly cover with wax paper.
Layer Cake, Frosted	about 17 oz.	Remove from package. Leave on styrofoam tray.	10 sec. Stand 15 sec. Cook 5 sec. Stand 1 min. Watch or icing will drip off.
Cheese Cake	about 17 oz.	Remove from foil container. Place on plate.	15 sec. Stand 15 sec. Repeat until cheese cake has cooked 1 min.
	1 serving	Place on plate.	20 sec. Stand 15 sec.

With ingenuity, a packaged cake mix can be disguised beyond recognition. To an ordinary mix, add wine, sour cream, fruit, vegetable, flavoring, gelatin, or pudding. Test the recipes in this book, and then try your own.

Basic Cake Mix

Follow the directions on the packaged cake mix, except add:

1 cup plus 1 tablespoon **water**
2 tablespoons **oil, mayonnaise, or sour cream**
2 eggs

1. Line baking dish with brown-in-paper or wax paper, lightly buttered, if you plan to remove the cake. If you plan to serve the cake in the container, butter the container.

2. Cook each cake uncovered, separately, except for cupcakes. You will have to experiment with time as each oven is different. Use a toothpick to test for doneness. It is better to slightly undercook the cake as it will continue to cook after removed from the oven.

Wine and Liquor

Exception to basic recipe: Use wine or other liquid instead of water. Use the wine by itself or added to any of the fruit recipes. For example, use strawberry wine to increase the flavor in the strawberry cake or add a white wine or sherry to the prune cake or applesauce cake.

Sour Cream

Exception to basic recipe: Use 3/4 cup of sour cream and 1/2 cup of water.

No oil.

Sour cream is good added to any of the nut, seed, and cereal recipes. Some of the vegetables and fruits will also combine beautifully with sour cream. Experiment with sour cream; try it in all of the recipes except the wine and liquor cakes.

Fruit

Exception to basic recipe: Use 3/4 cup of water. The liquid in the fruit makes up the balance. Be flexible and use your own judgment. Bake about 2 minutes longer for cupcakes and 3-5 minutes longer for regular recipe.

Vegetable

Exception to basic recipe: Use 3/4 cup of water. The liquid in the vegetable takes up the other 1/2 cup liquid. Be flexible and use your own judgment. Bake about 2 minutes longer for cupcakes and 3-5 minutes longer for regular recipe.

Flavoring

The following flavorings added to your cake will give it a lift: chocolate, anise, orange, chutney, cinnamon, coffee chocolate, and eggnog.

Apple Kuchen

1/4 cup **butter**, softened
3/4 cup **water**
3/4 **yellow cake mix**
1/2 cup **flaked coconut**
1 (20-ounce) can presliced **apples**, drained
1/2 cup **sugar**
1 teaspoon **cinnamon**
1 cup **sour cream**
1 **egg**, slightly beaten

1. Mix butter and water into dry cake mix.
2. Mix in coconut.
3. Spoon mixture into an ungreased oblong 12 x 7-inch pan. Cook 4 minutes, uncovered. Rotate every 60 seconds.
4. Arrange apple slices on warm crust.
5. Mix sugar and cinnamon. Sprinkle over apples.
6. Blend sour cream and egg. Pour over apples. (Topping will not completely cover apples.)
7. Cook 16 minutes, lightly covered with wax paper. Rotate 1/4 turn every 4 minutes.
8. Cool on wire rack for 10-15 minutes.

NOTE: Make 2 small kuchen if oven cavity is small.

Grandma Parson's Chocolate Cake From Scratch

2 cups **brown sugar**
1/4 cup **shortening**
1/2 cup **butter**
2 **eggs**, beaten
1/2 cup **sour milk** (See page 265.)
1/2 cup **water** plus 1 teaspoon **instant coffee**
1/2 cup **cocoa**
1/8 teaspoon **salt**
2 teaspoons **vanilla extract**
2 cups **flour**, sifted
1-3/4 teaspoons **baking powder**

1. In a bowl, cream sugar, shortening, and butter until light and fluffy.

2. Add eggs; blend. Add milk, coffee, cocoa, salt, and vanilla; stir until batter is smooth.

3. Sift flour and baking powder and add 1/2 cup at a time to the batter. Stir after each addition; blend.

4. Pour batter into two greased glass cake pans. Cook, uncovered, one layer at a time. See guide (page 198). Rotate 1/4 turn every 2 minutes.

5. Cool on wire rack for 10-15 minutes.

6. When cool, frost with a chocolate frosting.

Coca Cola Cake

1/2 pound **butter** or **margarine**
3/4 cup **Coca Cola**
1 **white cake mix**
1/4 cup **buttermilk**
2 **eggs**, beaten
1 teaspoon **vanilla extract**
1-1/2 cups **miniature marshmallows**

1. In a 1/2-quart container, cook butter and Coca Cola 3 minutes, uncovered.

2. In a bowl, blend the hot liquid into the cake mix.

3. Add buttermilk, eggs, and vanilla to the batter; stir until smooth.

4. Add marshmallows; stir.

5. Pour batter into two greased glass cake pans. Cook 7 minutes, uncovered, one layer at a time. Rotate 1/4 turn every 2 minutes.

6. Cool on wire rack for 10-15 minutes.

Frosting

1/4 cup **butter or margarine**
2 tablespoons **chocolate**
6 tablespoons **Coca Cola**
1 box **powdered sugar**
1 teaspoon **vanilla extract**

1. In a 1/2-quart container, bring butter, chocolate, and Coca Cola to a boil; cook 2 minutes, uncovered.

2. Pour mixture over the powdered sugar. Add vanilla. Blend until smooth.

3. Pour the warm frosting over the cake.

Graham Cracker Cake

1 **spice cake mix or applesauce cake mix**
2 cups **graham crackers, finely crushed**
1/3 cup **milk**
2 tablespoons **vegetable oil**
3/4 cup **water**
2 **eggs, beaten**
1 teaspoon **cinnamon**

1. In a bowl, combine all ingredients; stir until batter is smooth.

2. Pour batter into two greased glass cake pans. Cook, uncovered, one layer at a time. See guide (page 198). Rotate 1/4 turn every 2 minutes.

3. Cool on wire rack for 10-15 minutes.

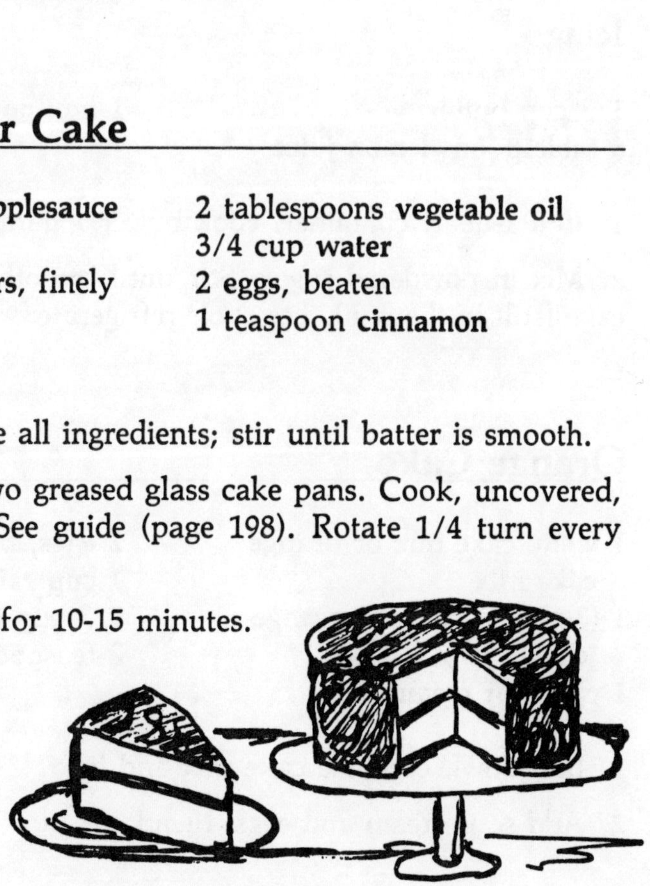

Lemon Cake

1 cup plus 1 tablespoon **water**
1 (3 3/4-ounce) box **instant lemon pudding**
1 **lemon cake mix**
2 **eggs**, beaten
2 tablespoons **vegetable oil**
1 teaspoon **lemon extract**

1. In a 1/2-quart container, cook water for 1 minute 30 seconds. Dissolve pudding in the hot water; stir; let cool.

2. In a bowl, combine the remaining ingredients; stir until smooth.

3. Add pudding mixture; blend.

4. Pour batter into two greased glass cake pans. Cook, uncovered, one layer at a time. See guide (page 198). Rotate 1/4 turn every 2 minutes.

5. Remove from oven; cool on wire rack for 10-15 minutes.

Icing

1/3 cup **butter**
6 tablespoons **lemon juice**
1 box **powdered sugar**

1. In a 1-quart container, cook butter 1 minute. Add lemon juice.

2. Mix in powdered sugar. Stir until smooth. Pour icing over hot cake (still in the pan). Let cool; refrigerate.

Orange Cake

1 **white cake mix** or **orange cake mix**
1 (3-ounce) package **orange jello**
1 cup **sour cream**
2 **eggs**, beaten
1 cup **raisins**, ground
1/3 cup **orange juice**
2 teaspoons dried **orange peel**

1. In a bowl, combine cake mix and jello.

2. Add sour cream and eggs; blend.

3. Add raisins, orange juice, and orange peel; stir until batter is smooth.

4. Pour batter into two greased glass cake pans. Cook, uncovered, 7-8 minutes one layer at a time. Rotate 1/4 turn every 2 minutes.

5. Cool on wire rack for 10-15 minutes.

Icing

1/2 cup **orange juice**	1/2 cup **sugar**

In a bowl, combine orange juice and sugar; blend. Pour over warm cake.

NOTE: Cake tastes better with fresh orange juice and 4 teaspoons fresh-grated orange peel.

Rhubarb Upside-Down Cake

3 cups fresh **rhubarb**, diced, or 1 (16-ounce) can **rhubarb**, undrained	1 cup **sugar**
1-1/2 cups **miniature marshmallows**	2 cups **biscuit mix**
	1 **egg**
	3/4 cup **water**
	1/3 cup **coconut** (optional)

1. Lay diced rhubarb in an 8 x 8 x 2-inch container. Add marshmallows and sprinkle 3/4 cup sugar over the top.

2. Combine the biscuit mix, 1/4 cup sugar, egg, water, and coconut; blend. Pour over rhubarb.

3. Cook 8-9 minutes, uncovered.

4. Cool on wire rack for 3-5 minutes. Turn cake upside down onto a platter.

NOTE: Cake tastes better with fresh rhubarb.

Poppy Seed Cake

1 pound cake mix
1/2 cup **poppy seeds**
butter (optional)

1. Prepare cake following mix directions.
2. Add poppy seeds; stir until batter is smooth.
3. Fill two greased glass loaf pans 1/2 full. Cook 7-9 minutes, uncovered. Rotate 1/4 turn every 2 minutes.
4. Cool on wire rack for 10-15 minutes.
5. Spread each slice with soft butter before serving.

Makes 2 loaves.

Sherry Cake

1 **yellow cake mix**
1 (3 3/4-ounce) package **instant vanilla pudding**
1 cup plus 1 tablespoon **sherry**
2 tablespoons **vegetable oil**
2 **eggs**, beaten
1 teaspoon **nutmeg**
1/3 cup **powdered sugar**

1. In a bowl, combine all ingredients except powdered sugar; stir until batter is smooth.
2. Pour into greased glass bundt pan. Cook 9-12 minutes, uncovered. Rotate 1/4 turn every 2 minutes.
3. Cool on wire rack for 10-15 minutes.
4. Sprinkle with powdered sugar.

NOTE: This can be prepared in two glass cake pans. Pour batter into two greased glass cake pans. Cook, uncovered, one layer at a time. See guide (page 198). Rotate 1/4 turn every 2 minutes.

Tunnel Cake

2 tablespoons **vegetable oil**
1 cup plus 1 tablespoon **water**
1 **chocolate cake mix**
2 **eggs**, beaten
1 (16 1/2-ounce) can **chocolate frosting mix**

1. In a bowl, combine oil, water, and chocolate cake mix.

2. Add eggs, one at a time; stir until batter is smooth.

3. Fold in 1/2 can chocolate frosting mix.

4. Pour into greased, glass bundt cake pan. Cook 10-12 minutes, uncovered. Rotate 1/4 turn every 2 minutes.

5. Cool on wire rack for 10-15 minutes. Frost with remaining mix.

NOTE: This can be prepared in two glass cake pans. Pour batter into two greased glass cake pans. Cook, uncovered, one layer at a time. See guide (page 198). Rotate 1/4 turn every 2 minutes.

White Cake and Orange Sauce From Scratch

2 cups **flour**
3/4 teaspoons **baking powder**
1/2 cup **shortening**
1 cup **sugar**
1 teaspoon **salt**
2 **eggs**, beaten
3/4 cup **milk**

1. Sift flour and baking powder 3 times. Set aside.

2. In a bowl, cream shortening, sugar, and salt until light and fluffy.

3. Add eggs; blend. Add milk; stir until batter is smooth.

4. Add flour mixture, 1/2 cup at a time, to the batter; stir after each addition.

5. Pour batter into two greased glass cake pans. Cook, uncovered, one layer at a time. See guide (page 198). Rotate 1/4 turn every 2 minutes.

6. Cool on wire rack for 10-15 minutes.

7. Pour sauce over hot or cool cake.

Orange Sauce

1 cup **orange juice**
1 cup **brown sugar**
2 tablespoons **flour**
2 tablespoons **butter**, melted

1. Combine juice, sugar, and flour; beat until smooth.

2. Cook 2-3 minutes, covered. Stir every 30 seconds. Add butter; stir.

Candies: Points to Remember

1. Most candies cook well in the microwave oven. You can also partially prepare candies in the microwave oven by just cooking parts such as chocolate pieces, marshmallows, and caramels.
2. Use a tall container that will tolerate a high temperature when candy mixture needs to boil.
3. When cooking candies that need to have the temperature taken, remove from the oven and then insert a candy thermometer into the hot mixture. NEVER COOK WITH A CANDY THERMOMETER IN THE MICROWAVE OVEN.
4. Stir candies often to keep from scorching.

Divinity

1 cup boiling **water**
1 cup **sugar**
1 cup **dark Karo syrup**
1/8 teaspoon **salt**
3 **egg whites**
1 teaspoon **vanilla extract**
1 cup **nuts**, chopped

1. Heat water in 2-quart container 3 minutes, uncovered.

2. Add sugar and Karo; stir. Cook 10 minutes, uncovered, or until it forms a fine thread when poured from a spoon.

3. Let stand 1 minute. Cook 30 seconds, uncovered. Remove from oven.

4. Add salt to egg whites. Beat until frothy.

5. Slowly add syrup to egg whites until mixture thickens and is dull; stir constantly. For best results use electric mixer.

6. Add vanilla and nuts.

7. Drop by teaspoonfuls on wax paper.

Makes 15-20 pieces.

Marshmallow Fudge

1 (13-ounce) can **evaporated milk**
4-1/2 cups **sugar**
3 bars **sweet German chocolate**
2 (12-ounce) packages **chocolate chips**
2 cups **marshmallow cream**
1/2 teaspoon **salt**
1 cup **nuts**, chopped
1-1/2 teaspoons **vanilla extract**

1. In a tall 4-quart container, heat milk 4 minutes. Add sugar; stir. Cook 2 minutes 30 seconds, uncovered. Stir every 30 seconds.

2. Add the rest of the ingredients in the order given; stir until melted. If needed, reheat for 30 seconds (optional).

3. Pour into an 8 x 8 x 2-inch buttered pan.

4. Cool and refrigerate 2 hours or until set. Cut in squares.

Makes 64 (1-inch) pieces.

Cookies: Points to Remember

1. Most bar cookies cook well in the microwave oven.
2. Lightly grease the bottom of the container only.
3. Do not cover bar cookies during cooking period.
4. Bar cookies do not brown on top.
5. When the cookies are done, moist areas may be on their surfaces. Additional cooking time does not help and may overcook inside.
6. To reduce the problem of a doughy center, elevate the cooking container. Set the filled glass container on an inverted plate (a glass 12-inch pizza plate works well).
7. Rotate container several times during cooking period.
8. Do not double recipes unless you cook each batch separately.
9. Toothpick test all cake-like bars, squares, and brownies. The bar, square, or brownie is done when toothpick inserted in the center comes out clean.
10. Individual cookies do not cook as well as bar cookies. The drier the batter the better they cook.
11. Refrigerate individual cookie dough batter at least one hour before using.
12. While still cool, roll refrigerated dough on a lightly floured board to one-eighth inch in thickness. Cut with a two-inch cookie cutter.
13. Add nuts to the outside of the cookies rather than to the dough mixture. Cookies cook unevenly around nut, chocolate chip, or other solid food ingredient mixed in the dough.
14. Cook individual cookies on a 12-inch pyrex glass pizza plate, or cut a piece of cardboard smaller than your oven cavity size and cover with wax paper. Cook nine cookies at a time arranged in a circular pattern.
15. Cook nine cookies 2 minutes to 2 minutes 30 seconds. Subtract 10 seconds per cookie if cooking less than nine cookies.
16. Heat room temperature cookies 15 to 20 seconds to make them warm or to freshen old cookies.

Cooky Convenience Foods Guide

Boxed

NAME	AMOUNT	DIRECTIONS	TIME
Brownies	15-17 oz.	Prepare according to pkg. directions. Place in 2-qt. greased baking dish (or line with wax paper). Rotate 1/4 turn every 2 min.	6-8 min., uncovered.
Date Bars	14 oz.	Cook dates.	2 min.
		Add dates to mix and prepare according to pkg. directions. Place in 2-qt. greased baking dish (or line with wax paper). Rotate 1/4 turn every 2 min.	6 min., uncovered.
Vienna Dreambars	12 oz.	Prepare according to pkg. directions. Place in 2-qt. greased baking dish (or line with wax paper). Rotate 1/4 turn every 2 min.	6 min., uncovered.

Frozen

NAME	AMOUNT	DIRECTIONS	TIME
Brownies, Frosted	13 oz.	Remove from foil container. Place on plate.	10 sec., uncovered.
Cookies or Unfrosted Brownie	1	Place on paper napkin.	30 sec., uncovered.

Refrigerated

NAME	AMOUNT	DIRECTIONS	TIME
Butterscotch, Peanut Butter, or Sugar Cookies	13 oz.	Let dough soften. While still cool, roll on a lightly floured cloth-covered board to 1/8-inch thickness. Cut with 2-inch cookie cutter.	2 min. to 2 min. 30 sec., uncovered, for 9 cookies. Subtract 10 sec. per cookie to cook less cookies.
		Cut a 9-inch square piece of cardboard. Cover with wax	Stand 30 sec.

NAME	AMOUNT	DIRECTIONS	TIME
		paper. Place 9 cookies on wax paper in a circular pattern, 2 inches apart, or use pyrex pizza plate.	
		Let stand and remove from wax paper with spatula.	

Almond Cookies

2-3/4 cups **flour**, sifted
3/4 cup **sugar**
dash **salt**
1 teaspoon **baking powder**
3/4 cup **butter**
2 **eggs** plus 1 **egg white**
1 teaspoon **cinnamon**
2 teaspoons **almond extract**
1 teaspoon **yellow food coloring** (optional)
1 **egg yolk**
1 tablespoon **water**

1. In a bowl, sift flour, sugar, salt, and baking powder.

2. In another bowl, combine butter, eggs, cinnamon, almond extract, and yellow food coloring. Batter will be coarse.

3. Add flour to mixture and knead on a lightly floured board.

4. Wrap in wax paper and refrigerate at least 1 hour.

5. Let dough soften outside refrigerator. While still cool, roll on a lightly floured board to 1/8-inch thickness. Cut with 2-inch cookie cutter.

6. Cut a 9-inch square piece of cardboard. Cover with wax paper. Arrange 9 cookies in a circular pattern, 2 inches apart or use pyrex pizza plate. Cook 2 minutes 30 seconds, uncovered.

7. Mix the egg yolk and water together. With a pastry brush, coat each cookie.

8. Cook 10 seconds, uncovered.

9. Let stand and remove from wax paper with a spatula.

Makes about 3-1/2 dozen cookies.

Brownies

2 eggs, beaten
1 teaspoon **vanilla extract**
1 recipe **brownie mix**
2/3 cup **nuts**, chopped

1. Prepare brownie mix.

2. In a bowl, blend all ingredients except nuts. Add nuts; stir (mixture will not be smooth).

3. Cook 6-8 minutes, uncovered, in a 7 x 12-inch, greased container. Rotate 1/4 turn every 2 minutes.

4. Cool 4 minutes on wire rack. Cut in squares. Remove and place on wax paper.

Mix

1/2 cup **flour**, sifted
1/4 teaspoon **baking powder**
1/4 teaspoon **salt**
1/2 cup **cocoa**, sifted
1 cup **sugar**
1/2 cup **shortening**

1. Sift into a large bag the flour, baking powder, salt, and cocoa.

2. Add sugar. Fold bag top and shake.

3. In a large bowl, pour ingredients from bag. Cut in shortening with pastry blender or 2 knives scissor-fashion.

4. Store mix in sack in a cool place until needed.

NOTE: Makes 1 recipe brownie mix.

Makes about 28 bars.

Applesauce Brownies

1 (1-pound 6-ounce) package **brownie mix**
3/4 cup **applesauce**
1/2 cup **nuts**, chopped
2 **eggs**, beaten

1. In a bowl, prepare brownie mix according to package directions except use applesauce for all the liquid. Blend until smooth.

2. Pour brownie batter into 7 x 12-inch container.

3. Cook 9 minutes 30 seconds, uncovered.

4. Cool on wire rack for 2 hours.

Makes about 28 bars.

Marshmallow Brownies

1 (6 1/2-ounce) package **fudge brownie mix**	1/4 cup **vegetable oil**
	2 cups **miniature marshmallows**

1. In a bowl, prepare brownies according to package directions except substitute 1/4 cup oil for part of the liquid. (Use water to make up the rest of the liquid.)

2. Pour into a 12 x 8 x 2-inch wax-paper-lined container.

3. Bake 5 minutes, uncovered. Toothpick test. Cook 1 minute more if wet in center.

4. Let stand on wire rack for 2 minutes. Remove from container and place upside down on wax paper. Sprinkle with miniature marshmallows immediately.

Topping

2-1/2 tablespoons **butter**	1 cup **powdered sugar**
3/4 cup **chocolate chips**	1 teaspoon **instant coffee**
3 tablespoons hot **water**	1/2 cup **nuts**, chopped

1. In a small container, cook butter and chocolate chips in water 1 minute 30 seconds, uncovered. Stir every 30 seconds.

2. Stir sugar, instant coffee, and nuts into chocolate sauce. Pour over marshmallow-covered brownies.

3. Cut in squares when cool.

Makes 10-12 servings.

Fast Dream Bars

1/2 cup **butter**
1/2 cup **brown sugar**
1 cup **flour**, sifted

1. In a bowl, cream butter with sugar until light and fluffy.
2. Add flour; blend.
3. Pat into a 12 x 7-inch wax-paper-lined container.
4. Cook 4-5 minutes uncovered. Rotate 1/4 turn every 60 seconds.
5. Let sit on wire rack for 2 minutes. Remove from container and place upside down on wax paper.
6. When cool, cover with topping and cut in squares.

Topping

1 (9 9/10-ounce) box **German chocolate cake icing mix**

In a bowl, prepare mix according to package directions.

Makes about 28 bars.

Graham Cracker Cookies

1 (6-ounce) package **chocolate chips**
12 **graham crackers**
1/2 cup **nuts**, chopped
1 cup **miniature marshmallows**

1. Place 1-1/2 tablespoons chocolate chips on each of 6 graham crackers.

2. Sprinkle nuts over top.

3. Place a few marshmallows on top of nuts.

4. Cook 1 minute, uncovered, on wax paper.

5. Press remaining graham crackers on the top. Cook 30 seconds, uncovered. Serve hot.

Makes 6 cookies.

NOTE: 1 cookie — cook 15-30 seconds
3 cookies — cook 30 seconds to 1 minute

Easy Graham Squares

4 tablespoons **butter**
1/2 cup **brown sugar**
2 eggs, beaten
3/4 cup **flour**, sifted
3/4 cup **graham cracker crumbs**
1/2 (1-pound 5-ounce) can **apple pie filling,** drained, chopped
3/4 cup **walnuts**, chopped

1. In a bowl, cream butter and sugar until light and fluffy; add eggs; stir.

2. Stir in flour, graham cracker crumbs, apple pie filling, and nuts.

3. Pour into an 8 x 8 x 2-inch container.

4. Cook 4 minutes, uncovered.

5. Cool 4 minutes on wire rack. Cut in squares. Remove and place on wax paper.

Makes 16 (2-inch) squares.

Icebox Cookies

1 cup **sugar**
1 cup **brown sugar**
1 cup **butter**
3 eggs, beaten
4 cups **flour**
1 teaspoon **soda**
1 teaspoon **salt**
1/2 teaspoon **vanilla extract**

1. In a bowl, cream sugar, brown sugar, butter, and eggs. Beat until smooth.

2. In another bowl, sift the flour with the soda and salt. Add to the above mixture, one cup at a time; stir.

3. Add vanilla; stir.

4. Wrap in wax paper and refrigerate for 6 hours or overnight.

5. When ready to use, let dough soften. While still cool, roll on a lightly floured board to 1/8-inch thickness. Cut with 2-inch cookie cutter.

6. Arrange 9 cookies on wax paper in a circular pattern, 2 inches apart, or use pyrex pizza plate. Cook 2 minutes 30 seconds, uncovered.

7. Let stand and remove from wax paper with a spatula.

Makes about 4 dozen cookies.

Easy Layer Cookies

1/2 cup **butter or margarine**
1-1/2 cups **graham cracker crumbs**
1 (6-ounce) package **chocolate chips**
1 (6-ounce) package **butterscotch chips**
1 cup **pecans, walnuts, or peanuts**, chopped
1 cup **shredded coconut**
1 (15-ounce) can **condensed milk**

1. In a 12 x 7-inch container, cook butter 1 minute, uncovered.

2. Layer the remaining ingredients pouring milk over all.

3. Cook 8-9 minutes, uncovered.

4. Let stand 10 minutes on a wire rack. Cut in bars. Remove and place on wax paper.

Makes about 28 bars.

Chocolate Peanut Brittle Bars

6 tablespoons **butter**
1 (6-ounce) package **chocolate chips or butterscotch chips**
1 (6 3/4-ounce) can **salted peanuts**
2-1/4 cups **sugar-coated rice cereal**

1. In a 12 x 7-inch container, cook butter and chocolate chips 3 minutes, uncovered. Stir every 30 seconds.

2. Add nuts and cereal. Stir to coat. Refrigerate until firm. Cut in squares.

Makes about 28 bars.

Pecan Bars

1 (8-ounce) can **crescent rolls**
1 **egg**, beaten
1/2 cup **pecans**, chopped
1/2 cup **sugar**
1/2 cup **corn syrup**
1 tablespoon **butter**, melted
1/2 teaspoon **vanilla extract**

1. Lightly grease a 12 x 7-inch glass container.

2. Separate crescent roll dough into rectangles. Press dough over bottom and 1/2 inch up the sides to form a crust. Cook 3 minutes, uncovered.

3. In a bowl, combine the rest of the ingredients.

4. Pour over crust and cook 7-9 minutes, uncovered. Rotate 1/4 turn every 2 minutes.

5. Cool 4 minutes on wire rack. Cut in bars. Remove and place on wax paper.

Makes 28 bars.

Brown Sugar Cookies From Scratch

1 cup **butter**
2 cups **brown sugar**
3 **eggs**, beaten
1 cup **sour cream**
4-1/2 cups **flour**
1/2 teaspoon **salt**
1 teaspoon **baking soda**

1. In a bowl, cream butter, sugar, eggs, and sour cream. Beat until smooth.

2. In another bowl, sift flour with salt and soda. Add to above mixture one cup at a time. Stir after each addition.

3. Add vanilla; stir.

4. Cover with wax paper and refrigerate 1 hour.

5. When ready to use, let dough soften. While still cool, roll on a lightly floured board to 1/8-inch thickness. Cut with 2-inch cookie cutter.

6. Cover a 9-inch square piece of cardboard with wax paper. Arrange 9 cookies in a circular pattern, 2 inches apart, or use pyrex pizza plate. Cook 2 minutes 30 seconds, uncovered.

7. Let stand and remove from wax paper with a spatula.

Makes about 50 cookies.

Fruits: Points to Remember

1. Most fruits cook well in the microwave oven.
2. Add sugar to fruit before cooking to help fruit to keep its shape.
3. Use brown sugar as topping for fruits.
4. Crumbled toppings over fruits become harder as they cool.
5. Most fruit desserts using a batter are cooked uncovered to allow moisture to escape.

Frozen Fruit Convenience Foods Guide

NAME	AMOUNT	DIRECTIONS	TIME
Frozen Fruit	10-oz. carton	Remove any metal or empty into serving dish or cook in plastic pouch.	1 min., covered.

Apple Compote

4 teaspoons **butter**
6 **apples**, peeled, cored, chopped
6 slices **whole wheat bread**, cubed
1 cup **raisins**
1 (8-ounce) can **pineapple tidbits**, drained
1/2 cup **flaked coconut**
1 cup **almonds** or **walnuts**
1/3 cup **white wine**

1. In a 3-quart container, cook butter 30 seconds, uncovered.

2. Add apples and bread. Cook 6 minutes, covered. Stir every 60 seconds.

3. Add all ingredients except wine. Cook 4 minutes, covered.

4. Add wine; stir. Let stand 5 minutes, covered.

Makes 4-6 servings.

NOTE: This is good with a pork roast.

Apple Dessert

8 **apples**, peeled, cored sliced
1/2 teaspoon **cinnamon**
1-1/2 teaspoons **apple pie spice**
1/2 teaspoon **salt**
1/2 cup **water**
1 cup **sugar**
3/4 cup **flour**
1/3 cup **butter**

1. In a 3-quart oblong container, add spices and water to apples.

2. Mix sugar and flour; cut in butter with a pastry blender or 2 knives scissor fashion. Spread over the apples like a crust.

3. Cook 10-12 minutes, lightly covered with wax paper. Rotate 1/4 turn every 2 minutes.

Makes 8 servings.

Apple Dumplings

1 (8-ounce) can refrigerated **biscuits**
1 or 2 **apples**, peeled, cored, cut in 1/2-inch square pieces
cinnamon
nutmeg
brown sugar

1. On a lightly floured board, roll out each biscuit 1/8 inch thick. Cut in 1-inch squares.

2. On half the dough squares, place a piece of apple. Sprinkle with cinnamon, nutmeg, and brown sugar. Top with remaining dough squares. Pinch together.

3. Make sauce.

4. In a 2-quart greased rectangular container, cover dumplings with sauce. Cook 6 minutes.

5. Brown in the microwave oven with browning element or conventionally.

Sauce

1 cup **white sugar**
2 cups **water**
4 tablespoons **butter**
2 teaspoons dried **orange peel**

In a 1-quart container, dissolve sugar in water. Add butter and orange peel. Cook 3 minutes, covered. Stir once.

Makes 4 servings.

Rum Bananas

3 tablespoons **lemon juice**
4 **bananas**, split lengthwise
3/4 cup **walnuts**, crushed
2 tablespoons **brown sugar**
1/2 teaspoon **nutmeg**
1/4 cup **rum**

1. Pour lemon juice over bananas and roll bananas in walnuts. Place in a small, shallow greased container.

2. Sprinkle bananas with brown sugar and nutmeg. Pour rum over the top.

4. Cook 4 minutes, uncovered. Rearrange twice during cooking period.

Makes 4 servings.

Fruit Cobbler

1/2 teaspoon **lemon juice**
1 (16-ounce) can **berries** or **peaches** or **apricots**, drained
3 tablespoons **butter**
1-1/2 cups **dry biscuit mix**
3 tablespoons **butter**, melted
1 **egg**, beaten
1/2 cup **milk**
Whipped cream or ice cream

1. Pour lemon juice over fruit. Dot with 3 tablespoons butter.

2. In a bowl, combine biscuit mix, butter, egg, and milk (should be crumbly).

3. Put fruit in a 7 x 12 x 2-inch greased container and pour biscuit batter over top.

4. Cook 10-12 minutes. Rotate 1/4 turn every 2 minutes. Brown in the microwave oven with browning element or conventionally.

5. Serve warm, topped with whipped cream or ice cream.

Makes 8-12 servings.

Hot Spiked Grapefruit

2 tablespoons **butter, melted**
2 **grapefruits,** cut in half, sectioned
1/2 cup **brown sugar**
4 **maraschino cherries**
1/4 cup **apricot brandy**

1. Pour melted butter over grapefruit.

2. Sprinkle brown sugar over each grapefruit half. Place a cherry in each center.

3. Place on wax paper; cook 3 minutes, uncovered.

4. Pour brandy over each half.

Makes 4 servings.

Large Peach Dumpling

4 fresh **peaches,** peeled, cored, cut in half
1 cup **champagne**
1 (8-ounce) package refrigerated **crescent rolls**

1. Soak peach halves in champagne for 1 hour; turn every 15 minutes.

2. Wrap each peach half in 2 dough triangles; prick dough with fork tines.

3. Cook 6-7 minutes, uncovered, on wax paper. Turn after first 4 minutes.

Makes 8 servings.

Baked Pears

4 tablespoons **lemon juice**
4 firm fresh **pears,** peeled, cored, halved
8 teaspoons **orange marmalade**
1/8 teaspoon **powdered ginger**
1 cup **raisins**
1 cup **almonds,** slivered
8 **maraschino cherries**
4 tablespoons **apricot jam**
2 tablespoons **water**
Fresh **mint leaves**
2 tablespoons **apple-mint jelly**

1. Pour lemon juice over pears in a shallow container.

2. Layer a portion of remaining ingredients except mint leaves and jelly in each cored part of pear.

3. Cook 10 minutes, loosely covered with wax paper, or until pears are done.

4. Garnish with fresh mint leaves and apple-mint jelly.

Makes 8 servings.

Pumpkin Compote

1 small, whole **pumpkin**
3 **apples,** peeled, cored, chopped
5 tablespoons **brown sugar**
4 tablespoons **butter**
1/2 teaspoon **cinnamon**
1/2 teaspoon **nutmeg**
1/2 cup **orange marmalade**
1/2 cup **sugar**
1-1/2 cups **nuts,** walnuts, pecans (They may be mixed or all one kind.)
1-1/2 cups **raisins**

1. Cut a small hole in the top of the pumpkin and remove seeds.

2. Bake 15 minutes without the lid.

3. Combine remaining ingredients. Pour into pumpkin cavity; cook 15 minutes. Place lid loosely on the top. Stir every 5 minutes (watch for steam).

Makes 4-6 servings.

NOTE: 1 (1-pound 13-ounce) can of pumpkin may be substituted. Pour into 3-quart container; cook 2 minutes, uncovered. Add the other ingredients and cook 15 minutes, covered. Stir 3 times.

Tapioca Apple Sausage

4 cups hot **water**
1 pound **sausage** links
7 **apples,** peeled, cored, sliced
3/4 cup **instant tapioca**
1 cup **brown sugar**

1. In a 2-quart container, cook 2 cups water 4 minutes, uncovered. Prick sausages; add them to the water. Let stand 2 minutes or more. Set aside.
2. In a 2-quart container, heat 2 cups water; cook 4 minutes. Add apples, tapioca, and brown sugar; stir. Press sausage down into mixture.
3. Cook 10-12 minutes, covered. Stir twice.

Makes 4-6 servings.

Icings and Toppings: Points to Remember

1. Most icings cook well in the microwave oven.
2. Stir icings frequently. They cook fast because of their high sugar content.
3. Cook dessert toppings as regular sauces. See page 42.

Icing and Topping Convenience Foods Guide

NAME	AMOUNT	DIRECTIONS	TIME
Canned Icing	1/2 jar	Cook in jar with lid removed.	45 sec., uncovered.
	more than 1/2 jar	2-cup measure or pitcher.	Add 30 sec. for every additional 1/2 jar.
Frozen, Whipped Icing	4-1/2 oz.	Remove cover.	Cook 5 sec., uncovered. Stir. Cook 5 sec., uncovered. Stir.

Caramel Icing

4 tablespoons **butter**, melted
1 cup **brown sugar**
1 cup **powdered sugar**
3 tablespoons **sour cream**
1/2 teaspoon **vanilla extract**

1. In a 1-quart container, combine butter, sugar, and sour cream. Cook 2 minutes, covered. Stir every 30 seconds.

2. Beat in sugar to spreading consistency. Add vanilla; stir.

Caramelizing

1 cup **sugar**

In a 3-quart rectangular container, cook sugar 4 minutes, uncovered. Stir every 30 seconds with rubber spatula or until sugar melts and turns brown.

Chocolate-Mocha Icing

4 tablespoons **butter**, melted
1 cup **sugar**
1/2 cup **cocoa**
2 teaspoons **instant coffee**
1/4 cup **milk**
1 teaspoon **vanilla extract**

1. In a 1-quart container, combine all ingredients except vanilla.

2. Cook 2 minutes, covered. Stir every 3 seconds.

3. Add vanilla; stir. Let stand 3 minutes; beat to spreading consistency.

Crumb Topping

3/4 cup **butter**
3/4 cup **sugar**
3/4 cup **brown sugar**
3/4 cup **flour**
3/4 cup **nuts,** chopped
1/4 cup **flaked coconut** (optional)

1. In a bowl, cream butter and sugars until light and fluffy; stir in flour.

2. Add nuts and coconut; stir.

3. Sprinkle on cake 2-3 minutes before done. (Part of the topping will sink into the cake.)

Flambé

1/4 cup **brandy**

1. In cup, cook brandy 20 seconds.

2. Ignite brandy and pour over food.

NOTE: Heat in cup and transfer to long-handled ladle before igniting.

Maple Icing

3 tablespoons **milk**
3/4 teaspoons **butter**
1/2 teaspoon **maple flavoring**
1-1/2 cups **powdered sugar**

1. In a cup or other small container, cook milk, butter, and maple flavoring 30 seconds, covered.

2. Pour over sugar. Beat to spreading consistency.

Peanut Butter-Marshmallow Icing

1 cup **sugar**
1 teaspoon **butter**
1/4 cup **cocoa**
1/3 cup **milk**
5 or 6 tablespoons **peanut butter**
2 cups **miniature marshmallows**
1 teaspoon **vanilla extract**

1. In a bowl, combine sugar, butter, cocoa, and milk; stir until smooth.

2. Pour into a 2-quart container and cook 5 minutes, covered. Stir every 30 seconds.

3. Add peanut butter, marshmallows, and vanilla; beat to spreading consistency.

Red Hot Cranberry Sauce

1 (16-ounce) can **jellied cranberry sauce**
1/2 cup **red hots candies**
3 **cinnamon sticks**

In a bowl, combine all ingredients. Cook 5 minutes, covered. Stir after first 3 minutes.

Makes 10-12 servings.

NOTE: This is good with a layer of cream cheese between two layers of refrigerated sauce:

1. Pour 1/2 cranberry sauce into a container; refrigerate until set.

2. Remove from refrigerator and add a layer of cream cheese.

3. Pour remaining cranberry sauce over cheese; refrigerate until set. Cut in squares.

Soft Custard Sauce

2 eggs, beaten
1 cup sugar
2/3 cup milk
4 tablespoons butter
1/4 teaspoon nutmeg
3 or 4 drops vanilla extract

1. In a bowl, combine all ingredients; stir until smooth.
2. Cook 4 minutes, uncovered. Stir every 30 seconds.
3. Pour over individual servings of desserts such as cake, ice cream, and fruit.

Makes 6-8 servings.

Pies

In old England, the first "pyes" were baked in a long, narrow, deep dish called a "coffin" or "pie receipt." The recipe books directed cooks, up to Martha Washington's day, to "first make your coffin." The round, shallow pie pans were designed to use less ingredients and to make the pie stretch further.

Pies: Points to Remember

1. Most pies cook well in the microwave oven.
2. Cook pie shell before adding filling. See page 231. This precooking keeps the crust from becoming soggy, yet there is no browning of pie shell.
3. When using boxed-mix pie dough or your own recipe, flute the edges higher than usual. This enables the shell to hold more filling and facilitates stirring the partially cooked pie filling.
4. Crumb toppings become harder as pies cool.
5. Cook cream fillings like puddings. See page 244.
6. Cook gelatin fillings to dissolve gelatin. See page 33.

7. When cooking a one-crust pie, such as custard or carrot, gently stir the outside edge of the filling to move cooked portion to the center. Stir after first three minutes cooking time.
8. To reduce the problem of a doughy bottom crust, elevate the filled glass pie plate on an inverted second pie plate or another plate.
9. Rotate pies one-quarter turn every two minutes.
10. After every two-minute cooking period, rest one minute. Repeat until pie is done. Most pies cook seven to nine minutes.
11. All frozen prepared pie shells can be substituted for your own recipe or a boxed pie dough mix. Frozen pie shells do not taste as good, but they are convenient and fast to use.
12. Meringue tops cannot be cooked in the microwave oven. Add meringue tops after pie has cooked and cook conventionally.

Pie Crust Guide

NAME	AMOUNT (CRUSHED)	BUTTER (MELTED)	TIME
Chocolate Cream Filled Cookies	1-1/2 cups	3-1/4 tablespoons	1 min. to 1 min. 30 sec.
Chocolate Wafers	1-1/2 cups	1/4 cup	1 min. to 1 min. 30 sec.
Coconut, Flaked or Shredded	2 cups	1/4 cup	2 min.
Gingersnaps	1-1/2 cups	1/3 cup	2 min.
Graham Crackers with 1/4 Cup Sugar	1 cup	1/3 cup	2 min.

Melt butter in a glass nine-inch pie plate. Add crushed cookies and sugar. Stir. Press mixture in bottom and up sides of pie plate.

Two Nine-Inch Solid Shortening Pie Crusts

1 teaspoon **salt**
2-1/4 cups sifted **all purpose flour**
3/4 cup **solid shortening** (no butter, margarine, or oil)
5 tablespoons **cold water**

1. In a large bowl, mix salt into flour.

2. Cut shortening into flour until the size of peas. (Use pastry blender or 2 knives scissor fashion.)

3. Blend 1/3 cup flour/shortening mixture with water. Add to rest of flour. Mix until dough holds together. Shape into a ball.

Two Nine-Inch Oil Pie Crusts

3/4 teaspoon **salt**
2 cups sifted **all purpose flour**
2/3 cup **vegetable oil**
1/3 cup boiling **water**

1. In a large bowl, mix salt into flour. Add oil. Mix with a fork until it looks like meal.

2. Slowly pour hot water into flour mixture. Mix with a fork until dough holds together. Shape into a ball.

Prepare Pastry

Prepare all pastry dough the same whether you start from scratch or use pie dough sticks or dry packaged mix.

Pie dough
2 (9-inch) **glass pie plates**
1 (8-inch) **glass pie plate**

1. On a floured board, roll out half of the dough for the first crust, about 1/8 inch thick and 1 inch larger than a 9-inch pie plate. (Be sure to dust rolling pin with flour.)

2. Round edges of pastry. Pinch together any broken edges. Fold the pastry in half and place in 9-inch pie plate. Unfold and ease pastry into pie plate. Do not stretch dough.

3. Flute edges flat with fork tines and prick bottom and sides of dough with fork tines.

4. Cover entire shell with paper towel. Place 8-inch pie plate inside the 9-inch pie shell, on top of the paper towel. Cook 3 minutes.

5. Remove 8-inch pie plate and paper towel. Cook 1 minute 30 seconds, uncovered.

6. Let stand 15-20 minutes before filling.

7. Repeat steps 1-6 to prepare second crust.

NOTE: Freeze commercially prepared pie shells for easy removal from foil container.

Pie Convenience Foods Guide

Room Temperature

NAME	AMOUNT	DIRECTIONS	TIME
Pie Slice	1 serving	Place on plate.	15 sec., uncovered.

Frozen

NAME	AMOUNT	DIRECTIONS	TIME
Cooked Cream Pie	8- to 9-inch pie	Remove from foil. Place in glass pie plate. Rotate pie 1/4 turn every 2 min.	10 sec. Stand 10 sec. Cook 10 sec. Stand 15 sec., uncovered.
Cooked Fruit Pie	8- to 9-inch pie	Remove from foil. Place in glass pie plate. Prick top crust with fork tines. Rotate pie 1/4 turn every 2 min.	5 min. Stand 1 min. Cook 3 min., uncovered. Brown in microwave oven with browning element or conventionally in a preheated 450° oven.
Uncooked Fruit Pie	8- to 9-inch pie	Remove from foil. Place in glass pie plate. Prick top crust with fork tines. Rotate pie 1/4 turn every 2 min.	13-16 min., uncovered. Brown in microwave oven with browning element or conventionally in a preheated 450° oven.

NAME	AMOUNT	DIRECTIONS	TIME
Uncooked Pie Shell	9-inch pie	Remove frozen pie shell from foil. Place in glass pie plate. Prick pie shell with fork tines.	Thaw 10 min.
		Cover entire shell with paper towel. Place 8-inch pie plate inside pie shell on top of paper towel.	Cook 6 min., uncovered.
		Remove 8-inch pie plate and paper towel.	Cook 1 min. 30 sec., uncovered.
		Let stand before filling.	Stand 15-20 min.
Cooked Pie Slice	1 serving	Place on paper plate.	Cook 15 sec., uncovered.

Almond Hershey Pie

1 **prepared pie shell**
1/2 cup **milk**
2 cups **miniature marshmallows**
6 **almond Hershey bars**, broken
3 tablespoons **creme de menthe or Kahlua**
1 cup **whipping cream**, whipped

1. Remove pie shell from foil container and place in a glass pie plate. See Prepare Pastry (page 231); start with step 4.

2. In a 1 1/2-quart container, combine milk, marshmallows, and broken pieces of Hershey. Cook 4 minutes, uncovered. Stir every 60 seconds.

3. Refrigerate 10 minutes.

4. Stir creme de menthe or Kahlua into whipped cream.

5. Fold Hershey mixture into whipped cream mixture and pour into cooled pie shell. Serve immediately or refrigerate.

American Apple Pie

2 sticks **pie dough mix**
1 cup **sugar**
2 tablespoons **flour**
1 teaspoon **apple pie spice** or
1/2 teaspoon **cinnamon** and
1/2 teaspoon **nutmeg**
6 or 7 **apples**, peeled, cored, sliced very thin
1-1/2 tablespoons **butter**
1/4 cup **rum** (optional)

1. Mix pie dough according to package directions. See Prepare Pastry (page 231).

2. In a large bowl, combine sugar, flour, and spices.

3. Add apples; stir to cover. Pour into pie shell and dot with butter. Pour rum over top.

4. Cover with top crust; prick with fork tines; flute edges.

5. Cook 2 minutes; rest 1 minute. Repeat until pie has cooked 8-9 minutes, uncovered. Rotate 1/4 turn every 2 minutes.

6. Brown in the microwave oven with browning element or conventionally.

7. Cool on wire rack.

Canned Apple Pie Filling

1 (1-pound 5-ounce) can **apple pie filling**

Follow American Apple Pie recipe except use apple pie filling.

Green Apple Pie

1-1/4 cup **sugar**
6 or 7 **green apples**, peeled, cored, sliced

Follow American Apple Pie recipe except use 1/4 cup more sugar and green apples.

French Apple Pie

1 prepared pie shell

1. Use American Apple Pie ingredients.

2. Remove pie from foil container and place in a glass pie plate. See Prepare Pastry (page 231); start with step 4.

3. Add pie filling.

4. Cook 4 minutes, uncovered. Gently stir around the edge to move cooked portion to the center.

5. Prepare crumb topping.

6. Sprinkle apples with crumb topping.

7. Cook 2 minutes; rest 1 minute. Repeat until pie has cooked 9-10 minutes. Rotate 1/4 turn every 2 minutes.

8. Cool on wire rack.

Crumb Topping

3/4 cup **brown sugar**
3/4 cup **butter**
1-1/4 cups **flour**

1. In a bowl, cream sugar and butter until light and fluffy.

2. In a bowl, cut butter mixture into flour until the size of peas with pastry blender or 2 knives scissor fashion.

NOTE: All apple pies are good served with cheese or topped with whipped cream or ice cream.

Mock Apple Pie

2 sticks **pie dough mix**
16 **soda crackers,** quartered
1/2 teaspoon **cinnamon**
1/2 teaspoon **apple pie spice**
2 tablespoons **butter**
1-1/3 cups **water**
1-1/3 cups **sugar**
1 teaspoon **cream of tartar**

1. Mix pie dough according to package directions. See Prepare Pastry (page 231).

2. Spread out quartered crackers on bottom of pie shell. Sprinkle with spices and dot with butter.

3. In a 1-quart container, combine water, sugar, and cream of tartar; stir. Cook 3 minutes, uncovered, or until boiling. Pour over crackers.

4. Cover with top crust; prick with fork tines; flute edges.

5. Cook 2 minutes, uncovered; rest 1 minute. Repeat until pie has cooked 8-9 minutes. Rotate 1/4 turn every 2 minutes.

6. Brown in the microwave oven with browning element or conventionally.

7. Cool on wire rack.

Canned Berry Pie

2 sticks **pie dough mix**
1 cup **sugar**
5 tablespoons **flour**
3/4 teaspoon **cinnamon**
1 (1-pound 5-ounce) can **berries,** drained
1-1/2 tablespoons **lemon juice** (Use with mild-flavored berries only.)
1-1/2 tablespoons **butter**

1. Mix pie dough according to package directions. See Prepare Pastry (page 231).

2. In a 1-quart container, combine the sugar, flour, and cinnamon.

3. Add the canned berries and lemon juice; gently mix.

4. Pour berry filling into pie shell. Dot with butter.

5. Cover with top crust; prick with fork tines; flute edges.

6. Cook 2 minutes, uncovered; rest 1 minute. Repeat until pie has cooked 7-8 minutes. Rotate 1/4 turn every 2 minutes.

7. Brown in the microwave oven with browning element or conventionally.

8. Cool on wire rack.

Fresh Berry or Fruit Pie

2 sticks **pie dough mix**
1-1/2 cups **sugar**
1/3 cup **flour**
3/4 teaspoons **cinnamon**
4 cups fresh **berries** or other **fruit**
2 tablespoons **butter**
1-1/2 tablespoons **lemon juice** (Use with mild-flavored berries only.)

1. Mix pie dough according to package directions. See Prepare Pastry (page 231).

2. In a large bowl, combine sugar, flour, and cinnamon.

3. Add berries or other fruit and lemon juice; gently mix.

4. Pour fruit filling into pie shell. Dot with butter.

5. Cover with top crust; prick with fork tines; flute edges.

6. Cook 2 minutes, uncovered; rest 1 minute. Repeat until pie has cooked 8 minutes. Rotate 1/4 turn every 2 minutes.

7. Brown in the microwave oven with browning element or conventionally.

8. Cool on wire rack.

Carrot Pie

1 **prepared pie shell**
1-1/2 cups **carrots,** cooked, mashed
1 cup **brown sugar**
1/8 teaspoon **salt**
1 teaspoon **cinnamon**
1 teaspoon **ginger**
1/8 teaspoon **allspice**
2 tablespoons **honey** or **molasses**
3 **eggs,** beaten
1 cup **evaporated milk**

1. Remove pie shell from foil container and place in glass pie plate. See Prepare Pastry (page 231); start with step 4.

2. In a bowl, combine all ingredients; beat until smooth.

3. Pour carrot filling into pie shell.

4. Cook 3 minutes, uncovered. Gently stir around the edge to move cooked portion to the center.

5. Cook 2 minutes, uncovered; rest 1 minute. Repeat until pie has cooked 8-9 minutes. Rotate 1/4 turn every 2 minutes.

6. Cool on wire rack.

Cherry or Blueberry Pie

1 **prepared pie shell**
1 (3-ounce) package **cream cheese**
1/2 cup **sugar**
1 teaspoon **vanilla extract**
1 cup **whipping cream,** whipped
1 (1-pound 5-ounce) can **cherry** or **blueberry pie filling,** some of the syrup drained off

1. Remove pie shell from foil container and place in a glass pie plate. See Prepare Pastry (page 231); start with step 4.

2. In a bowl, combine cream cheese, sugar, and vanilla. Fold in whipping cream.

3. Pour filling over mixture.

4. Serve immediately or refrigerate.

Cherry-Mincemeat Pie

1 prepared **pie shell**
1 (1-pound 5-ounce) can **cherry pie filling**, some of the syrup drained off
1 (9-ounce) package **mincemeat**
1 tablespoon **minute tapioca**

1. Remove pie shell from foil container and place in a glass pie plate. See Prepare Pastry (page 231); start with step 4.

2. In a bowl, combine filling, mincemeat, and tapioca; let stand 20 minutes.

3. Pour into pie shell.

4. Cook 3 minutes, uncovered. Gently stir around the edge to move cooked portion to the center.

5. Cook 2 minutes, uncovered; rest 1 minute. Repeat until pie has cooked 7-8 minutes. Rotate 1/4 turn every 2 minutes.

6. Cool on wire rack.

German Chocolate Pie

1 prepared **pie shell**
1 (4-ounce) package **German chocolate**, broken
1/3 cup **butter**
1 cup **evaporated milk**
1-1/4 cups **sugar**
4 tablespoons **cornstarch**
1/8 teaspoon **salt**
2 **eggs**, beaten
1 teaspoon **vanilla extract**
1 cup **flaked coconut**
1/4 cup **pecans**, chopped

1. Remove pie shell from foil container and place in a glass pie plate. See Prepare Pastry (page 231); start with step 4.

2. In a 11/2-quart container, melt chocolate and butter. Cook 2 minutes, uncovered. Stir every 30 seconds. Blend in milk.

3. In a bowl, combine sugar, cornstarch, and salt; stir in eggs and vanilla. Add flaked coconut and pecans; stir.

4. Slowly blend in the chocolate mixture; stir until smooth.

5. Pour mixture into pie shell and cook 3 minutes, uncovered. Gently stir around the edge to move cooked portion to the center.

6. Cook 2 minutes, uncovered; rest 1 minute. Repeat until pie has cooked 6-7 minutes. Rotate 1/4 turn every 2 minutes.

7. Cool on wire rack and let stand 3 hours.

Cranberry-Eggnog Pie

1 prepared **pie shell**
1 (16-ounce) can **jellied cranberry sauce**
6 tablespoons **water**
2 tablespoons **unflavored gelatin**
1-3/4 cups **commercial eggnog**
2 tablespoons **rum**
1/8 teaspoon **nutmeg**
1/2 cup **whipping cream,** whipped

1. Remove pie shell from foil container and place in a glass pie plate. See Prepare Pastry (page 231); start with step 4.

2. Spread cranberry sauce over bottom of cooled pie shell.

3. In a cup, combine water and gelatin. Cook 1 minute, uncovered. Stir after first 30 seconds.

4. Pour eggnog into a 1-quart container; add dissolved gelatin, rum, and nutmeg; stir.

5. Cook 2 minutes, uncovered. Stir every 30 seconds. Let cool 10 minutes; stir twice.

6. Fold cream into eggnog and pour over cranberry mixture. Refrigerate 2 hours or until firm.

Cream of Wheat Pie

1 prepared **pie shell**
8 **eggs,** beaten
3 cups **sugar**
1/2 cup **butter**
1/2 cup **water**
3 tablespoons **cream of wheat** or other **creamed cereal**
1-1/2 teaspoons **vanilla extract** or other flavoring
1/2 cup **nuts,** chopped

1. Remove pie shell from foil container and place in glass pie plate. See Prepare Pastry (page 231); start with step 4.

2. In a bowl, combine all ingredients; beat until smooth.

3. Pour filling into pie shell.

4. Cook 3 minutes, uncovered. Remove from oven. Gently stir around the edge to move cooked portion to the center.

5. Cook 2 minutes, uncovered; rest 1 minute. Repeat until pie has cooked 9-10 minutes. Rotate 1/4 turn every 2 minutes.

6. Cool on wire rack.

Peanut Butter Pie

1 **prepared pie shell**
1/2 cup **brown sugar**
3 **eggs**, beaten
1 cup **light corn syrup**
1 teaspoon **vanilla extract**
1/8 teaspoon **salt**
3/4 cup **chunky peanut butter**
1/2 cup **chocolate chips**
1/4 cup **coconut**, flaked

1. Remove pie shell from foil container and place in glass pie plate. See Prepare Pastry (page 231); start with step 4.

2. In a bowl, combine sugar and eggs; stir.

3. Add corn syrup, vanilla, salt, and peanut butter. Blend until smooth. For best results, use electric mixer.

4. Pour filling into pie shell and cook 3 minutes, uncovered. Gently stir around the edge to move cooked portion to the center.

5. Cook 2 minutes, uncovered; rest 1 minute. Repeat until pie has cooked 7-8 minutes. Rotate 1/4 turn every 2 minutes.

6. Sprinkle chocolate chips and flaked coconut over the top of the hot pie.

7. Cool on wire rack 20 minutes.

Indian Ginger-Pear Pie

1 **prepared pie shell**
2 (16-ounce) cans **pears,** sliced, drained, or 4 cups **fresh pears,** sliced
3/4 cup **sugar**
2-1/2 teaspoons **ginger**
3 tablespoons **instant tapioca**

1. Remove pie shell from foil container and place in a glass pie plate. See Prepare Pastry (page 231); start with step 4.

2. In a bowl, combine pears, sugar, ginger, and tapioca; let stand 20 minutes.

3. Make crumb topping and set aside.

4. Pour pear filling into pie shell. Cook 3 minutes, uncovered. Gently stir around the edge to move cooked portion to the center.

5. Add crumb topping. Cook 2 minutes, uncovered; rest 1 minute. Repeat until pie has cooked 7-8 minutes. Rotate 1/4 turn every 2 minutes.

6. Cool on wire rack.

Crumb Topping

1/2 cup **butter**
1 cup **flour**
3/4 cup **brown sugar**

1. In a bowl, cut butter into flour until size of peas with pastry blender or 2 knives scissor fashion.

2. Add sugar and stir.

Pecan Pie

Crust

1 cup **graham cracker crumbs**
1/4 cup **pecans,** chopped
4 tablespoons **butter,** melted
3 tablespoons **sugar**

Combine crust ingredients and press into a 9-inch glass pie plate.

Filling

1 (8-ounce) package **cream cheese**, softened
2 **eggs**, beaten
1 cup **sugar**
1/2 teaspoon **vanilla extract**
1/4 teaspoon **salt**
3 tablespoons **flour**, sifted
2 teaspoons **lemon peel**, grated, or 1 teaspoon dried **lemon peel**
2 tablespoons **lemon juice**
1/2 cup **pecans**, chopped
1/2 cup **whipping cream**

1. In a large bowl, combine all ingredients except whipping cream; beat until smooth. For best results, use electric mixer.

2. Add whipping cream. Stir until blended into mixture. Pour into pie shell.

3. Cook 3 minutes, uncovered. Gently stir around the edge to move cooked portion to the center.

4. Cook 2 minutes, uncovered; rest 1 minute. Repeat until pie has cooked 6-7 minutes. Rotate 1/4 turn every 2 minutes.

5. Cool on wire rack; refrigerate.

Pumpkin Pie

1 **prepared pie shell**
1 (16-ounce) can **pumpkin**
2 cups **milk**
1-1/2 cups **sugar**
2 tablespoons **dark corn syrup**
3 **eggs**, beaten
1 teaspoon **cinnamon**
1 teaspoon **pumpkin pie spice**
1/8 teaspoon **salt**

1. Remove pie shell from foil container and place in glass pie plate. See Prepare Pastry (page 231); start with step 4.

2. In a bowl, combine all ingredients; beat until smooth.

3. Pour into pie shell.

4. Cook 3 minutes, uncovered. Gently stir around the edge to move cooked portion to the center.

5. Cook 2 minutes, uncovered; rest 1 minute. Repeat until pie has cooked 9-10 minutes. Rotate 1/4 turn every 2 minutes.
6. Cool on wire rack.

Puddings and Custards: Points to Remember

1. Cook cream-type puddings in a four-cup measure, uncovered.
2. Stir cream-type puddings often. You can keep a wooden spoon in pudding during cooking period.
3. To cook most other puddings, cook two minutes, loosely covered with wax paper, and stir. Then cook four minutes, and gently stir around edge to move cooked portion to the center. Cook four minutes more, loosely covered with wax paper.
4. Custards must cook just below the boiling point.
5. Set custard-filled container inside a second container filled with about one inch of hot water.
6. Watch custards carefully. They cook at different rates, depending on your oven cavity size and microwave pattern.
7. Most custards cook in eight to ten minutes.
8. Custard is done when inserted knife comes out clean.
9. For a soft custard sauce, see page 229.

Pudding and Custard Convenience Foods Guide

NAME	AMOUNT	DIRECTIONS	TIME
Custard Mix	4-1/2 oz.	In a 1-qt. container, prepare according to pkg. directions. Sprinkle with nutmeg. Set filled container inside large container (with about 1 inch hot water).	2 min., loosely covered with wax paper. Stir. Cook 4 min., uncovered. Stir around edge to move cooked portion to center. Cook 4 min., uncovered.

NAME	AMOUNT	DIRECTIONS	TIME
Danish Dessert Pudding and Pie	4 oz.	Place in 1 1/2-qt. container. Pour in 2 cups water or fruit juice and mix. Stir every 30 sec.	4 min. to 5 min. 30 sec., uncovered.
Frozen Pudding	17-1/2 oz.	Place covered plastic carton in oven. Stir twice.	1 min., uncovered. Stir. Cook 45 sec., uncovered. Stir.
Individual Puddings	1 container	Remove foil. Cook in slit plastic pkg.	15 sec.
Pudding Mix	3 oz.	In a 1-qt. container, prepare according to pkg. directions. Stir every 30 sec.	4 min. to 5 min. 30 sec., uncovered.

NOTE: For extra goodness, pour 1/2 teaspoon maple syrup into the bottom of each custard cup before pouring in hot custard.

Custard

2-1/4 cups **milk**, scalded
4-5 **eggs**, beaten
1/3 cup **sugar**
1/8 teaspoon **salt**
1/2 teaspoon **vanilla extract**
Nutmeg

1. In a 1-quart measure, cook milk 3 minutes 30 seconds to 4 minutes.

2. In a bowl, combine all ingredients except nutmeg and pour into a 11/2-quart container. Sprinkle with nutmeg.

3. Set filled container inside a larger container with about 1 inch hot water.

4. Cook 4-5 minutes, uncovered.

Makes 4-6 servings.

Grapenut Custard

2 cups **milk**
1 cup **grapenuts**
3/4 cup **sugar**
3 **eggs**, beaten
1/8 teaspoon **salt**
1/2 teaspoon **vanilla extract**

1. In a 1-quart measure, cook milk 3 minutes 30 seconds to 4 minutes.

2. In a bowl, combine all ingredients and pour into 6 (5-ounce) custard cups.

3. Cook 4 minutes to 5 minutes 30 seconds. Remove when custard bubbles.

Makes 4-6 servings.

Milk-Rice Custard

2 cups **milk**
2 **eggs**, beaten
1/2 tablespoon **butter**
1/2 cup **sugar**
1/2 cup **quick-cooking rice**
1/8 teaspoon **salt**
1 teaspoon **vanilla extract**
1/4 teaspoon **nutmeg**
1/4 teaspoon **cinnamon**

1. In a 1-quart container, cook milk 3 minutes, uncovered.

2. In a 1/2-quart container, combine the remaining ingredients. Add hot milk; stir.

3. Set filled container inside a larger container with about 1 inch hot water. Cook 2 minutes, uncovered. Stir. Cook 4 minutes. Gently stir around edge to move cooked portion to the center.

4. Cook 4 minutes or until knife inserted near center comes out clean.

5. Cool on a wire rack; refrigerate or serve immediately.

Makes 6-8 servings.

Apple-Oatmeal Pudding

4 apples, peeled, cored, sliced thin
3/4 cup **brown sugar**
1/4 teaspoon **cinnamon**
1/4 cup **sugar**
1/3 cup **butter**
1 egg, beaten
1/2 teaspoon **vanilla extract**
1/2 cup **quick-cooking oats**
1-1/2 tablespoons **baking powder**
1/8 teaspoon **salt**
1/2 cup **flour**
1/2 cup **milk**

1. In a 2-quart greased container, sprinkle apples with brown sugar and cinnamon.

2. In a bowl, cream sugar and butter until light and fluffy. Add egg and vanilla; blend. Pour over apples.

3. In a bowl, combine oats, baking powder, salt, and flour.

4. Alternating twice, add the oat mixture and milk to the sugar mixture.

5. Cook 2 minutes, loosely covered with wax paper; stir. Cook 4 minutes. Gently stir around edge to move cooked portion to the center. Cook 4 minutes, loosely covered.

Makes 4-6 servings.

Berry or Fruit Pudding

1 cup **sugar**
1-1/2 cups **flour**, sifted
1 teaspoon **baking powder**
1/8 teaspoon **salt**
1 cup **milk**
2 tablespoons **butter**
2 cups any **fruit** or **berry**
1 cup **sugar**
2 cups hot **water**

1. In a deep 3-quart container, combine sugar, flour, baking powder, salt, milk, and 1 tablespoon butter. Pat down smooth.

2. Place fruit or berries on top of dough mixture and sprinkle with sugar. Add hot water. Dot with 1 tablespoon butter.

3. Cook 2 minutes, loosely covered with wax paper. Stir. Cook 4 minutes. Gently stir around edge to move cooked portion to the center. Cook 4 minutes, loosely covered.

Makes 4-6 servings.

Chocolate Bread Pudding

2 cups **milk**
4 tablespoons **butter**
3-1/2 cups soft **bread crumbs**
1/2 cup granulated **brown sugar**
3 **eggs**, beaten
1/4 teaspoon **salt**
1/2 cup **chocolate chips**

1. In a 1-quart measure, combine milk and butter. Cook 3 minutes 30 seconds.

2. In a 7 x 12-inch container, combine all ingredients.

3. Set filled container inside a larger container with about 1 inch hot water.

4. Cook 2 minutes, uncovered. Stir. Cook 4 minutes. Gently stir around edge to move cooked portion to the center. Cook 4 minutes, loosely covered.

Makes 6-8 servings.

NOTE: To make bread pudding, omit the chocolate and add 1/3 cup raisins, 1/3 teaspoon cinnamon, and 1/3 teaspoon nutmeg.

Cream Pudding

1/2 cup **sugar**
2 tablespoons **unflavored gelatin**
1/8 teaspoon **salt**
2 cups **milk**
4-5 **egg yolks**, beaten
1 cup **whipping cream**, whipped
1 teaspoon **vanilla extract**

1. Combine sugar, gelatin, salt, milk, and egg yolks in a 1-quart measure.
2. Cook 4 minutes 30 seconds to 5 minutes. Stir every 2 minutes.
3. Place container in cold water.
4. When cool, fold in whipped cream and vanilla.
5. Pour into a 1-quart mold or other container and refrigerate until set.

Variations

Butterscotch

1/2 cup **butterscotch chips**

Add before cooking.

Chocolate

1/2 cup **chocolate chips**

Add before cooking.

Mocha Cream

3 tablespoons **instant coffee**

Add before cooking.

Peppermint

1/4 teaspoon **peppermint flavoring**

Add instead of vanilla.

Makes 6-8 servings.

Graham Cracker Pudding

1 pound **graham crackers,** crumbled
2 cups **brown sugar**
1/4 cup **raisins**
1/4 cup **walnuts,** chopped
1 **egg,** beaten
1 cup **water**
2 teaspoons **baking powder**
1/8 teaspoon **salt**
1 teaspoon **rum flavoring** or **vanilla extract**

1. In a 2-quart greased container, combine all the ingredients; blend until smooth.

2. Cook 2 minutes, loosely covered with wax paper. Stir. Cook 2 minutes. Gently stir around edge to move cooked portion to the center. Cook 2 minutes, loosely covered.

Makes 6-8 servings.

Ozark Pudding

2 cups **apples,** diced
1 cup **nuts,** chopped
3/4 cup **flour,** sifted
2 cups **sugar**
1/8 teaspoon **salt**
3/4 teaspoon **baking powder**
4 tablespoons **rum**

1. In a 11/2-quart greased container, combine all the ingredients.

2. Cook 2 minutes, loosely covered with wax paper; stir. Cook 4 minutes. Gently stir around edge to move cooked portion to the center. Cook 2 minutes, loosely covered.

Makes 4 servings.

Russian Pashka

3 cups small-curd **cottage cheese**
5 tablespoons **butter,** room temperature
1-1/4 cups **whipping cream**
3 **egg yolks**
3/4 cup **sugar**
1/8 teaspoon **nutmeg**
1/8 teaspoon **cinnamon**
1/3 cup **candied fruit,** chopped
1/2 cup **almonds,** chopped

1. In a 1 1/2-quart container, combine cheese and butter.

2. In a bowl, beat cream, egg yolks, sugar, nutmeg, and cinnamon until smooth. Slowly blend in cream. Add to cheese mixture.

3. Cook 2 minutes, loosely covered with wax paper. Stir. Cook 4 minutes. Gently stir around edge to move cooked portion to the center. Cook 4 minutes, loosely covered.

4. Fold in fruit and almonds. Place container in a bowl of ice cubes; stir gently. When cool, press mixture into a buttered mold. Refrigerate.

Makes 6-8 servings.

Tapioca Pudding

3-1/2 tablespoons **minute tapioca**
6 tablespoons **sugar**
1/8 teaspoon **salt**
1-1/2 cups **milk**
2/3 cup **cream**
1 **egg,** separated
1/2 teaspoon **vanilla extract** or **almond flavoring**

1. In a 1 1/2-quart container, combine tapioca, 4 tablespoons sugar, salt, milk, cream, and egg yolk; blend. Let stand 5-6 minutes.

2. Cook 5-1/2 minutes, covered. Stir every 60 seconds. (Tapioca mixture must come to a boil.)

3. Stir in flavoring; let stand 2 minutes.

4. Beat egg white until frothy. Add 3 tablespoons sugar. Fold egg white mixture into tapioca pudding. Let stand 10-15 minutes, covered.

5. Serve hot or cold.

Makes 4 servings.

Fast Zabaglione Custard

1-1/4 cups **milk**
1 **egg yolk**
1/2 teaspoon dried **lemon peel**
1 (3-ounce) package **custard mix**
6 tablespoons **Marsala or sherry wine**

1. In a 2-quart container, combine milk, egg yolk, lemon peel, and custard mix; blend.

2. Set filled container inside a larger container with about 1 inch hot water.

3. Cook 3 minutes, uncovered. Gently stir around edge to move cooked portion to the center.

4. Add wine; cook 1-2 minutes, uncovered.

5. Cool on a wire rack; refrigerate or serve immediately.

Makes 4 servings.

JAMS & JELLIES

Because home canned items taste better and save money, home canning has increased in popularity. Our spirits lift a little when we serve foods we've canned ourselves.

An old recipe, dated before 1870, from *Recipes, Remedies and Reflections* by Harry Emerick, instructs the housewife "to gather a desired amount of ripe persimmons in the fall, after the first frost or so. These are then taken into the house. . . ." No recipes like that are listed here, but if you want to pick your own fruit, then your jams and jellies will hold a sweet memory. My sons Shawn and Todd picked wild plums in the sandhills of northwest Oklahoma with their grandmother. Stained hands and dirty clothes were a sure sign of the fun they had had. The plum recipe on page 255 is the one used to make jam from these tiny, tart plums.

Jams and jellies can be easily prepared in the microwave oven because they don't have to reach the jellying point or be vacuum sealed.

When the jam or jelly is ready, ladle it quickly into hot, sterilized jars or glasses. To help keep air bubbles from forming, hold the ladle close to the jar opening. Fill the glasses almost to the top, and cover with paraffin, which should touch all edges. Prick any air bubbles that form. Let stand until paraffin hardens and turns white.

Cover with wax-paper lids by cutting circles larger than the jar top and securing them with rubber bands. Store in a cool place.

Apricot Jam

1 (8-ounce) can **pineapple,** diced, drained
1-1/2 (6-ounce) bottles liquid **pectin**
3-1/2 cups fresh **apricots,** skinned, pitted, cut in pieces
5 cups **sugar**

1. In a 3-quart container, combine all ingredients except sugar; stir.
2. Refrigerate overnight.
3. Cook 8 minutes, uncovered. Stir once.
4. Add sugar; stir to dissolve.
5. Cook 6 minutes, uncovered. Stir every 30 seconds. Skim with slotted spoon.
6. Pour into hot sterilized jars; cover with paraffin immediately.

Makes about 1 quart.

Peach Jam

12 **peaches,** peeled, cut in pieces
1 **orange,** peeled, white removed, cut in small pieces
2 (6-ounce) bottles liquid **pectin**
6 cups **sugar**

1. In a 3 1/2-quart container, combine all ingredients except sugar; stir.
2. Let stand 2 hours.
3. Cook 15 minutes, uncovered. Stir twice.
4. Add mashed sugar; stir to dissolve.
5. Cook 20 minutes, uncovered. Stir every 5 minutes. Skim with slotted spoon.
6. Pour into hot sterilized jars; cover with paraffin immediately.

Makes about 2 quarts.

Plum Jam

4 cups **plums,** washed, pitted
1 (6-ounce) bottle liquid **pectin**
3 cups **sugar**

1. In a 3-quart container, place whole plums. Cover with water. Cook 9 minutes, covered.
2. Drain water; remove skins.
3. Mash plums; add pectin; stir.
4. Cook 8 minutes, uncovered. Stir once.
5. Add sugar; stir to dissolve.
6. Cook 6 minutes, uncovered. Stir every 2 minutes. Skim with slotted spoon.
7. Pour into hot sterilized jars; cover with paraffin immediately.

Makes about 1 quart.

NOTE: Wild plums and beach plums are good in this recipe.

Strawberry Jam

4 cups **strawberries,** washed
1 (6-ounce) bottle liquid **pectin**
5 cups **sugar**

1. In a 3-quart container, mash strawberries. Add pectin; stir.
2. Cook 8 minutes, uncovered. Stir once.
3. Add sugar; stir to dissolve.
4. Cook 6 minutes, uncovered. Stir every 2 minutes. Skim with slotted spoon.
5. Pour into hot sterilized jars; cover with paraffin immediately.

Makes about 1 quart.

Spiced Apple Jelly

4 cups canned unsweetened **apple juice**
1 (6-ounce) bottle liquid **pectin**
5 cups **sugar**
2 sticks **cinnamon,** broken into pieces
16 **cloves**

1. In a 3-quart container, combine apple juice and pectin; stir.
2. Cook 8 minutes, uncovered. Stir once.
3. Add sugar; stir to dissolve.
4. Cook 6 minutes, uncovered. Stir once. Skim with slotted spoon.
5. Place a few pieces of cinnamon stick and a few cloves in each hot sterilized jar.
6. Pour mixture into jars; cover with paraffin immediately.

Makes about 1 quart.

Wine Jelly

4 cups **wine**
1 (6-ounce) bottle liquid **pectin**
5 cups **sugar**

1. In a 3-quart container, combine wine and pectin; stir.
2. Cook 8 minutes, uncovered. Stir once.
3. Add sugar; stir to dissolve.
4. Cook 6 minutes, uncovered. Stir once. Skim with slotted spoon.
5. Pour into hot sterilized jars; cover with paraffin immediately.

Makes about 1 quart.

Three Flavors Marmalade

1-1/2 cups **carrots**, grated
2-1/2 cups **rhubarb**, ground
2 whole **oranges**, ground
1-1/2 (6-ounce) bottles liquid **pectin**
1/4 cup **lemon juice**
5 cups **sugar**

1. In a 4-quart container, combine all ingredients except sugar; stir.
2. Cook 11 minutes, uncovered. Stir once.
3. Add sugar; stir to dissolve.
4. Cook 10 minutes, uncovered. Stir twice. Skim with slotted spoon.
5. Pour into hot sterilized jars; cover with paraffin immediately.
6. Keep refrigerated.

Makes about 1-1/2 quarts.

Cranberry-Orange Relish

1 pound **cranberries**, ground
1 large **orange**, ground
Rind from 1/2 **orange**, ground
1 (6-ounce) bottle liquid **pectin**
3 cups **sugar**

1. In a 3-quart container, combine all ingredients except sugar.
2. Cook 8 minutes, uncovered. Stir once.
3. Add sugar, stir to dissolve.
4. Cook 6 minutes, uncovered. Stir every 2 minutes. Skim with slotted spoon.
5. Pour into hot sterilized jars; cover with paraffin immediately.

Makes a little over a quart.

Pineapple Relish

3 tablespoons **onion,** chopped
2 tablespoons **butter**
1 (8-ounce) can **pineapple,** crushed
4 tablespoons dried **parsley flakes**
1-1/2 teaspoons **prepared mustard**

1. Cook onion in butter 1 minute, uncovered. Stir every 30 seconds.

2. Add the remaining ingredients. Cook 2 minutes, covered. Stir every 30 seconds.

3. Keep refrigerated.

Makes about 3/4 cup.

REFERENCE

GLOSSARY

Au Gratin	To top with a crust of grated cheese, or a combination of cheese and bread crumbs, and brown
Bake, Meat	See guide (page 92).
Bake, Vegetable	To cook vegetable in oven in microwave cooking
Barbecue	To spoon sauce over meat and cook uncovered
Baste	To moisten food while it is cooking to keep surface from drying and to add flavors
Beat	To stir food vigorously with a rhythmic motion, using a fork, spoon, whisk, handbeater, or electric mixer
Blanch	To immerse food in boiling water to remove the skin
Blend	To make a uniform mixture of two or more ingredients
Boil	To cook food in water or liquid that has reached 212 degrees Fahrenheit by direct heat.
Broil	To cook food over hot coals or under direct heat. You cannot broil in the microwave oven. (Sear meat conventionally, then reduce time by cooking in the microwave oven.)

Brown	To cook food under high heat until it turns brown
Caramelize	To slowly heat sugar until it melts and turns golden brown (See page 226.)
Chill	To refrigerate food until it becomes cold
Chop	To cut food in small pieces or bits with a knife
Coat	To cover the top layer of foods evenly with a food mixture
Combine	To blend together all ingredients
Cook	To heat food in microwave cooking
Cool	To let food stand at room temperature until the item is no longer hot
Cream	To beat one or more food items until they are thoroughly mixed
Cube	To cut food in small squares
Cut in	To cut shortening into flour by using a pastry blender or two knives scissor fashion until approximately the size of small peas
Deep-fat Fry	Do not deep-fat fry in the microwave oven because the oil does not remain at a constant temperature.
Dice	To cut in very small segments
Dissolve	To mix a dry ingredient with a liquid until the dry ingredient melts and becomes part of the liquid
Dot	To scatter small pieces of butter or margarine on another food ingredient
Dredge	To coat with flour
Flake	To easily separate cooked fish with a fork
Flambé	To cover food with warmed liquor that is ignited just before serving (See page 227.)

Fold In	To gently combine two ingredients by immersing one ingredient into the other with a spoon, spatula, or wire whisk and then carefully turning the mixture over
Garnish	To add a small or decorative food item as an accompaniment
Grate	To shred food by rubbing it against a food grater
Grease	To coat inside of cooking container with butter, margarine, or shortening
Knead	To mix and work dough with hands
Loosely Cover	To place a piece of wax paper or paper towel over a cooking container without tightness
Marinate	To soak food in a liquid, acidic mixture before cooking
Melt	To change food from a solid to a liquid state by heating it uncovered
Mince	To cut food in very fine pieces
Pan-Broil	To cook uncovered in a hot skillet and pour off fat as it accumulates. You cannot pan-broil in microwave cooking. (Pan-broil conventionally, then reduce time by cooking in the microwave oven.)
Pan-Fry	To cook uncovered in a skillet using a small amount of oil. You cannot pan-fry in microwave cooking. (Pan-fry conventionally, then reduce time by cooking in the microwave oven.)
Peel	To cut away outer covering
Poach	To cook food in simmering liquid (In microwave cooking, the food item and liquid, in a cooking container, are covered tightly in plastic wrap.)
Puree	To liquefy food in an electric blender or press it through a sieve

Roast	To cook a large piece of meat. See guide (page 92).
Sauté	To fry food lightly in a small amount of oil, stirring frequently and cooking uncovered
Scald	To heat a liquid near the boiling point
Sear	To brown the surface of meat using the microwave browning platter (See broil.)
Simmer	To cook liquid, or food in liquid, to just below the boiling point, cooking covered and turning the microwave oven off every few minutes to keep the liquid from boiling
Skewer	To secure meat and other food items with a thin rod
Steam	To cook in hot-water vapor by placing a small amount of water in a container with food item and tightly covering with plastic wrap before putting in the microwave oven
Steep	To submerge food in boiling water (No other cooking is necessary.)
Stir	To mix food by passing a spoon or fork through it in a circular motion
Toast	Bread will not toast in the microwave oven, but it may be reheated there. See guide (page 184).
Toss	To mix lightly until well coated with a dressing
Whip	To beat into a froth with a spoon, fork, whisk, hand beater, or electric mixer to increase air and volume

EQUIVALENTS

Substitutions

Baking Powder	1 teaspoon (for leavening) = 1/4 teaspoon baking soda plus 1/2 teaspoon cream of tartar
Chocolate	1 square unsweetened chocolate = 1/4 cup cocoa
Cornstarch	1 tablespoon = 2 tablespoons flour
Egg	8 to 10 egg whites = 1 cup 12 egg yolks = 1 cup
Flour	1 cup cake flour = 1 cup less 2 tablespoons all purpose flour 1 tablespoon = 1/2 tablespoon cornstarch or 2 teaspoons quick-cooking tapioca (for thickening only)
Garlic	1/8 teaspoon garlic powder = 1 clove garlic 3/4 teaspoon garlic salt = 1 clove garlic and dash of salt
Herb	1 teaspoon dry = 1 tablespoon fresh
Honey	1 cup = 3/4 cup sugar plus 1/4 cup any liquid
Milk	1 cup = 1/2 cup evaporated milk plus 1/2 cup water 1 cup = 1 cup dry milk plus 2 tablespoons butter 1 cup sour milk = 1 cup milk plus 1 tablespoon white vinegar or lemon juice

Equivalents Onion	1 tablespoon chopped or minced onion = 1 medium onion or 1/4 cup
Pepper	1 tablespoon sweet pepper flakes = 2 tablespoons chopped fresh pepper
Vegetable	1 tablespoon vegetable flakes = 3 tablespoons chopped fresh vegetables

Weights and Measures

Dash	=	1/8 teaspoon or less
3 teaspoons	=	1 tablespoon
4 tablespoons	=	1/4 cup
5-1/3 tablespoons	=	1/3 cup
8 tablespoons	=	1/2 cup
16 tablespoons	=	1 cup
16 fluid ounces	=	2 cups
1 cup	=	1/2 pint
2 cups	=	1 pint
4 cups	=	1 quart
4 quarts	=	1 gallon
16 ounces	=	1 pound

INDEX